Complete Horoscope

Aries 2023

Monthly astrological forecasts for 2023

TATIANA BORSCH

Translated from Russian by Sonja Swenson
Translation copyright © Coinflow Limited, Cyprus
AstraArt Books is an imprint of Coinflow limited, Cyprus
Published by Coinflow Limited, Cyprus
For queries please contact: tatianaborsch@yahoo.com
ISBN978-9925-579-97-6(paperback)
ISBN 978-9925-579-98-3(ebook)

Contents

2023 – The Great Transition Continues 5

2023 Overview for Aries 11

January 14

February 17

March 20

April 23

May 26

June 29

July 32

August 35

September 38

October...................................41

November 44

December 47

Aries Description 50

A Guide to The Moon Cycle and Lunar Days...................................55

A Guide to Zodiac Compatibility 84

Love Description of Zodiac Signs...................................92

2023 – The Great Transition Continues

In previous forecasts, I have described the unique transition period in which the world finds itself.

I will summarize for those who have not read my predictions for 2020, 2021, and 2022.

We have entered a period of changes, and the world has come to a fateful point, where everything that seemed constant and unshakable no longer is. If that is the case, then what awaits us?

From an astrological perspective, 2020, 2021, and 2022 are extensions of one long period, and cannot be divided. This is a time of major changes in every nation, home, and individual.

There is no comparison for this period in modern history. In fact, humanity has not lived through a period quite like this for a very long time.

The astrological explanation for this is that we are living through a grandiose shift in eras. The Age of Pisces, which lasted for 2,160 years, is transitioning into the Age of Aquarius.

2023 fits naturally into this complex sequence. This is an important and critical watershed.

During the first half of 2023, we see a natural continuation of a very complicated period that began in 2022. The confrontation between East and West will continue in Ukraine, as will rivalry between the United States and China, along with financial and economic crises that have beset the entire world.

As of June 2022, when this forecast is being written, I can predict that in the fall of 2022, that is in October and November, the conflict between Russia and the West in Ukraine will reach a new level. Russia's advancements will force the West, including the United States, to take on a more active role in the face of the invasion in Ukraine, as the entire world risks being dragged into a new war.

The stars predict that the war in Ukraine may come to an end in January-February 2023. Ukraine will be divided into two zones of influence, with much of its territory falling under Russia's shadow. Volodymyr Zelenskyy will lose his grip on power and may flee the country, and Ukrainian leadership will be replaced. Peace initiatives that might otherwise be capable of changing this tragic situation will constantly be thwarted. In January 2023, aggressive Mars will no longer be in retrograde, and by February, there will be a light at the end of the tunnel. Initially, it will be just a flicker, but it is certainly better than nothing.

Gradually, the countries involved in this conflict will come to realize that they need to hold constructive negotiations in order to meet all of society's healthy demands and trends. These talks will not be swift, and they will probably only bear fruit in the second half of 2023.

Overall, despite Ukraine's valiant efforts both militarily and politically, along with support from the West, Russia will prevail, militarily, geopolitically, and ideologically.

This will seriously alter the geopolitical landscape on the global stage. In time, Asia and Russia will dominate the world's economy. The events of this year are just one more step in the transition as global influence shifts eastward. Tensions between the United States and Asian countries will only heat up.

In late 2022 and early 2023, many countries' economies will descend into chaos, and a general financial crisis will drag down banks, companies, and the entire planet's population.

In many Western countries, antiwar sentiment will be palpable, and there may be demonstrations, protests, and other expressions of dissatisfaction with governments.

In Russia, the fall of 2022 and first half of 2023 will see widespread changes in the structures of power. Western sanctions will lead to serious economic losses, forcing Russia to find a way to survive in the face of Western and American economic aggression.

The worst economic crisis will take place in the United States. The fall of 2022 and during the first half of 2023 may be the worst period it has faced in recent memory. There may be serious confrontations between political parties, which might throw American society as a whole off balance. During the fall of 2022 and first half of 2023, President Biden will experience serious difficulties. The stars predict he will face worsening health, along with serious destabilization of the entire American financial system. (A president's horoscope is responsible for much of what will happen to his or her country). During the same period, Bident's great foe, former President Trump, is expected to become much more active and powerful.

European countries will not be spared, either. In France, opposition to President Macron's policies will grow and Macron will lose some of his influence.

In Germany, Chancellor Olaf Scholz will become more aggressive during the fall. Despite his outward calm, he may turn out to be an active supporter of Western support for Ukraine. This will lead to a backlash in German society, and by May 2023, Scholz will be in a much weaker position than he is today.

From November 2022 to May 2023, the United Kingdom may see changes in leadership. This will be a period full of obstacles, including serious financial difficulties, demonstrations by those who disagree with the political power structure, and a trend of separatism in the various regions. In June-July, things will calm down significantly, and the British financial and political system will manage to recover.

The second half of May will also be a time of challenges. Jupiter will square Pluto during this time, with support from aggressive Mars. We can expect cataclysms and changes in many countries' governments here. Serious acts of terrorism cannot be ruled out, either.

During the second half of 2023, Jupiter will transition from the bellicose sign of Aries into the more peaceful sign of Taurus, and its favorable aspect with Saturn in June gives reason to hope that things are likely to improve.

That process will not be overnight, however. We see evidence of that in Uranus, which will be in the sign of Taurus, at the same degrees as during the period of World War II. Taurus symbolizes life and all its peaceful manifestations, while Uranus is the symbol of renewal through destruction. That portends a break with old structures, which may unleash war, death, and political and economic clashes.

All of these painful processes will eventually lead to the birth of a new, modern world, but that will not be completed until after 2025.

Looking at the future, I predict that in late 2022, and early 2023, economic, political, and social, as well as personal crises will reach a peak. Remember, we are blessed to live in an era of great change, and historical events certainly do leave their mark on our personal lives.

I also predict that during the second half of 2023, we will reach the halfway point on this long and winding road, and this may be the most complicated part of that trajectory. After this point, people will begin looking for a way to resolve the world's most pressing problems, and the light at the end of the tunnel may start to glimmer a bit brighter. Of course, this is inevitable, but step by step, people will start to tackle the many challenges we face. This is a gradual, sometimes painful process. But there is hope that Fate will have less unpleasant surprises in store for us and life will start running a bit more smoothly. It will never go back to exactly the way it was, but as this period draws to a close, we will see that in one way or another, all of these changes are for the best.

Money

We may face a global banking system crisis, which is likely to happen in November-December 2022. I believe it would be wiser to hold your money in something tangible, like real estate, land, or gold, than in the banking system or simply on paper. Purchasing power may experience a serious decline.

Health

Health-wise, anyone with thyroid problems or cardiovascular disease or any illnesses involving the blood vessels of the brain should be particularly cautious. We see this as Uranus transits into Taurus.

Pluto is still in Capricorn, which exacerbates musculoskeletal and bone disorders. Teeth are also in Pluto's crosshairs, so it is best to treat them quickly!

Cancer cases may rise, so do not hesitate to visit the doctor quickly, as cancer is only treatable in the early stages.

In 2023, Saturn is transiting into Pisces – this may lead to problems for those with various types of diabetes or problems involving the legs.

During the spring and fall of 2023, more outbreaks of unknown diseases and viruses are possible.

Nature

In 2023, various natural anomalies that the world has been struggling with may continue. Jupiter in Aries might cause fires, which will be a destabilizing factor during the winter and spring of 2023.

However, in early May, when Jupiter transitions into Taurus, we can expect to see significant improvements in agriculture. Harvests will be more abundant, which, in many countries, will mean a way out of the food crisis. Many countries will also be able to invest more in agriculture production and processing, which will only revive small towns and villages.

Fashion

Jupiter will be in Aries during the first half of 2023, and this promises all shades of red, which will be on models everywhere during this period. Many people will instinctively be drawn to red, as Aries's energy simply hangs in the air. Military-inspired dress may also be on the runways.

During the second half of 2023, Jupiter will transition into Taurus, which is primarily green in color. This is a great color, as it symbolizes growth and rebirth. Taurus's second color is pink, which symbolizes romanticism, softness, love for sensual pleasures and enjoyment. The fashion world may respond in kind with light, floaty fabrics and perhaps a new focus on femininity.

Have a wonderful year! Don't be afraid of crises, as they bring with them new opportunities!

Always,

Tatiana Borsch

2023 Overview for Aries

You are embarking on a brilliant, productive year. Jupiter, the planet of success, is on your side, which means that it's now or never!

Work. After a difficult and unpredictable 2022, you are on the upswing again at work. Most likely, you will start to notice this in February, and it will be marked by several important events.

Your ruler, Mars, will start to move on a straight path, and your life will start to see a process of renewal, progress, and breaks with the past. Slowly but surely, you may resume contact with colleagues in other cities or abroad and revitalize a past partnership. Things are unlikely to run smoothly, but the road belongs to those who walk it, and in the end, things will work out.

Starting in May, you will start a new chapter at work. Both business owners and managers may see changes related to expanding their business and additional income.

During the second half of the year, be attentive to the demands of your business partners or certain opponents. You may run into serious disagreements over money and overcoming that will be no easy task. The stars recommend that you steel yourself for any claims against you and get your documents in order, especially those related to finances. Be ready for any audits, as well.

During the first half of 2023, from February to May, employees may receive new responsibilities or a promotion right where you are, which will significantly improve your financial situation.

Money. Overall, 2023 is a fairly positive time for your bank account. Most Aries will have an opportunity to improve their material situation, which is reflected in all other areas of your life, as well.

The best months of the year for you are January, the second half of May, June, the second half of September, and December.

Most of your expenses will take place in August, the second half of October, and November. They may be directly related to business, or possibly matters involving your family or home.

Love and family. Your personal life can be divided into different halves. During the first half, you will enjoy stability and predictability, which will be replaced by turbulent passions during the second half.

Couples on the rocks will have to deal with challenges once again, and this time, they will involve money or other material items. This is especially likely during the fall and winter of 2023 – October, November, and December. You may be discussing divorce, but that only applies if you have had a longstanding grudge with one another. There may be a love triangle involved, and you will be forced to make a choice.

Couples who get along might be focused on major construction projects, and closer to the fall, they may invest a lot of resources into this. One partner will be in agreement with this, and the other will not. Naturally, that will lead to arguments, which will begin in October and November, but be over by the holidays.

Single people have a great chance of meeting their better half in 2023, and acquiring real estate, as well.

Health. Much of the year, you will enjoy the support of Jupiter, which is a powerful source of energy, meaning that you have no reason to fear falling ill. However, during the difficult autumn, in October and November, it is worth being attentive to your body and avoiding any injuries, while also being more careful behind the wheel.

If you are elderly or weakened by chronic disease, take care, because there is a high likelihood of a recurrence. Take protective measures, and if you need it, seek the advice of a doctor.

January

New York Time			London Time		
Calendar Day	Lunar Day	Lunar Day Start Time	Calendar Day	Lunar Day	Lunar Day Start Time
01/01/2023	11	12:58 PM	01/01/2023	10	12:31 PM
02/01/2023	12	1:32 PM	02/01/2023	11	12:56 PM
03/01/2023	13	2:10 PM	03/01/2023	12	1:27 PM
04/01/2023	14	2:53 PM	04/01/2023	13	2:05 PM
05/01/2023	15	3:42 PM	05/01/2023	14	2:51 PM
06/01/2023	16	4:36 PM	06/01/2023	15	3:45 PM
07/01/2023	17	5:32 PM	07/01/2023	16	4:45 PM
08/01/2023	18	6:31 PM	08/01/2023	17	5:50 PM
09/01/2023	19	7:30 PM	09/01/2023	18	6:56 PM
10/01/2023	20	8:29 PM	10/01/2023	19	8:04 PM
11/01/2023	21	9:28 PM	11/01/2023	20	9:11 PM
12/01/2023	22	10:28 PM	12/01/2023	21	10:19 PM
13/01/2023	23	11:29 PM	13/01/2023	22	11:28 PM
15/01/2023	24	12:32 AM	15/01/2023	23	12:40 AM
16/01/2023	25	1:38 AM	16/01/2023	24	1:54 AM
17/01/2023	26	2:47 AM	17/01/2023	25	3:11 AM
18/01/2023	27	3:56 AM	18/01/2023	26	4:28 AM
19/01/2023	28	5:05 AM	19/01/2023	27	5:42 AM
20/01/2023	29	6:08 AM	20/01/2023	28	6:46 AM
21/01/2023	30	7:02 AM	21/01/2023	29	7:38 AM
21/01/2023	1	3:55 PM	21/01/2023	1	8:55 PM
22/01/2023	2	7:49 AM	22/01/2023	2	8:17 AM
23/01/2023	3	8:28 AM	23/01/2023	3	8:48 AM
24/01/2023	4	9:01 AM	24/01/2023	4	9:13 AM
25/01/2023	5	9:32 AM	25/01/2023	5	9:34 AM
26/01/2023	6	10:01 AM	26/01/2023	6	9:54 AM
27/01/2023	7	10:30 AM	27/01/2023	7	10:14 AM
28/01/2023	8	11:00 AM	28/01/2023	8	10:35 AM
29/01/2023	9	11:33 AM	29/01/2023	9	11:00 AM
30/01/2023	10	12:10 PM	30/01/2023	10	11:29 AM
31/01/2023	11	12:52 PM	31/01/2023	11	12:04 PM

You can find the description of each lunar day in the chapter "A Guide to The Moon Cycle and Lunar Days"

You recently went through a difficult period, but it seems that there is a light at the end of the tunnel. As always, you can keep your head held high!

Work. During the first 20 days of January, you will be busy with work and the holidays will be but a memory.

Entrepreneurs and managers will be able to conclude a difficult period at work, which may have been caused by colleagues from other cities or abroad, or possibly unresolved legal problems.

Despite all the setbacks, during the last ten days of the month, the sky will clear – you are on the right track and victory will be yours. You can lean on your close partners, old friends, and most importantly, Jupiter, which is now on your side.

After January 12, when your ruler, Mars, finally begins moving in a straight line, you will find an opportunity to reach a smooth path of prosperity and development. Your relationships with colleagues from other cities or abroad, which may have been shaky in the past, will improve considerably.

After lengthy negotiations, employees might count on a promotion or an entirely new job. You can be sure of protection from old friends or mentorship from someone highly placed in society. In any case, you might not get what you want this month, but soon – from February to April – things will go your way. January is just a springboard for improvements and development later on.

Money. When it comes to finances, January is looking pretty good. Though you are spending a lot, you have more money than expenses and will be able to cover it all.

Expect to receive the greatest sums on January 1, 2, 11, 12, 21, 22, 28, and 29. Many of your expenses will take place during the second half of the month, but they will be predictable and reasonable.

Love and family. You can count on improvements in all areas of your personal life in January. Difficult situations with relatives are coming to a favorable resolution.

In many situations, this may involve relatives living in other cities or abroad, and your relationships are slowly improving.

You might also find yourself back in the arms of an old flame who now lives far away, or perhaps an old friend. You can expect things to become clearer during the last 10 days of January and all of February.

Health. January is one of the best months for you, energy-wise. You are healthy, full of vitality, and ready to climb mountains.

The only downside this month is meeting challenges while traveling and behind the wheel. The trickiest period is during the first 20 days of the month.

If you want to travel somewhere far from home, be very careful with your documents and following the law in other countries. Better yet – pick a destination where you have been before, in order to avoid any nasty surprises.

February

New York Time		
Calendar Day	Lunar Day	Lunar Day Start Time
01/02/2023	12	1:38 PM
02/02/2023	13	2:30 PM
03/02/2023	14	3:26 PM
04/02/2023	15	4:24 PM
05/02/2023	16	5:23 PM
06/02/2023	17	6:22 PM
07/02/2023	18	7:22 PM
08/02/2023	19	8:22 PM
09/02/2023	20	9:22 PM
10/02/2023	21	10:24 PM
11/02/2023	22	11:27 PM
13/02/2023	23	12:33 AM
14/02/2023	24	1:40 AM
15/02/2023	25	2:46 AM
16/02/2023	26	3:50 AM
17/02/2023	27	4:47 AM
18/02/2023	28	5:36 AM
19/02/2023	29	6:19 AM
20/02/2023	1	2:09 AM
20/02/2023	2	6:55 AM
21/02/2023	3	7:28 AM
22/02/2023	4	7:58 AM
23/02/2023	5	8:28 AM
24/02/2023	6	8:59 AM
25/02/2023	7	9:32 AM
26/02/2023	8	10:08 AM
27/02/2023	9	10:49 AM
28/02/2023	10	11:34 AM

London Time		
Calendar Day	Lunar Day	Lunar Day Start Time
01/02/2023	12	12:48 PM
02/02/2023	13	1:39 PM
03/02/2023	14	2:37 PM
04/02/2023	15	3:41 PM
05/02/2023	16	4:47 PM
06/02/2023	17	5:54 PM
07/02/2023	18	7:02 PM
08/02/2023	19	8:10 PM
09/02/2023	20	9:19 PM
10/02/2023	21	10:28 PM
11/02/2023	22	11:40 PM
13/02/2023	23	12:54 AM
14/02/2023	24	2:09 AM
15/02/2023	25	3:22 AM
16/02/2023	26	4:28 AM
17/02/2023	27	5:24 AM
18/02/2023	28	6:09 AM
19/02/2023	29	6:44 AM
20/02/2023	1	7:09 AM
20/02/2023	2	7:11 AM
21/02/2023	3	7:35 AM
22/02/2023	4	7:56 AM
23/02/2023	5	8:16 AM
24/02/2023	6	8:38 AM
25/02/2023	7	9:02 AM
26/02/2023	8	9:30 AM
27/02/2023	9	10:03 AM
28/02/2023	10	10:44 AM

You can find the description of each lunar day in the chapter "A Guide to The Moon Cycle and Lunar Days"

You do what you think you need to do, and follow your heart, too. But there's no better feeling than when both things coincide!

Work. The various challenges you took on in 2022 are either resolved or close to a favorable end. You are once again turning to things you had put off and making future plans. You are sure to see positive, long-term, and impressive results.

Right now, you have support from many people, and you are looking for the right people, new partners, and renewing old ties in February.

Difficult relationships with colleagues in other cities or abroad will finally become predictable this month. You might even have constructive negotiations and a successful trip. You are likely to pick up some old partnerships too, right where you left off.

By turning to some old friends for support, employees find themselves accomplishing remarkable things. That means either a promotion where you are or an entirely new job. Hold onto your hats! Your time has come!

The best time for any work-related events is from February 1 to 23. The last week of the month will be less active and better for reflecting on everything you have learned.

Money. Financially speaking, February is a time of ups and downs and contradictions. You will have money, but there are no escaping expenses. There is not much you can do to avoid this. After all, change is never free.

If you are not part of the working world and do not have your own business, you will find yourself spending many of your resources on friends, loved ones, and children. Keep in mind that your expenses this month will be useful, and even pleasurable.

Love and family. Your family situation is also stabilizing. Thorny issues related to your relatives are nearly resolved, and you might take a trip and see family members who live in other cities or abroad.

Minor disagreements are likely during the first 10 days of February, but they will be favorably resolved in the second half of the month.

Couples can expect some hiccups during the first 10 days of the month. Some old wounds may rear their heads again, and you will be forced to get to the very root of your problems. You will manage, though you should try to manage any personal issues with kid gloves. Of course, that advice is good any time, especially for you!

Single people can expect a fateful encounter, and it is most likely to take place while you are traveling or among people from far away.

Health. During February, you are healthy, energetic, and ready to move mountains. During the last few days of the month, however, all the hecticness may finally catch up with you, leaving you feeling fatigued.

March

New York Time			London Time		
Calendar Day	Lunar Day	Lunar Day Start Time	Calendar Day	Lunar Day	Lunar Day Start Time
01/03/2023	11	12:24 PM	01/03/2023	11	11:33 AM
02/03/2023	12	1:19 PM	02/03/2023	12	12:29 PM
03/03/2023	13	2:16 PM	03/03/2023	13	1:31 PM
04/03/2023	14	3:15 PM	04/03/2023	14	2:36 PM
05/03/2023	15	4:15 PM	05/03/2023	15	3:44 PM
06/03/2023	16	5:14 PM	06/03/2023	16	4:52 PM
07/03/2023	17	6:15 PM	07/03/2023	17	6:00 PM
08/03/2023	18	7:15 PM	08/03/2023	18	7:09 PM
09/03/2023	19	8:17 PM	09/03/2023	19	8:19 PM
10/03/2023	20	9:20 PM	10/03/2023	20	9:31 PM
11/03/2023	21	10:25 PM	11/03/2023	21	10:44 PM
13/03/2023	22	12:31 AM	12/03/2023	22	11:58 PM
14/03/2023	23	1:37 AM	14/03/2023	23	1:11 AM
15/03/2023	24	2:40 AM	15/03/2023	24	2:18 AM
16/03/2023	25	3:37 AM	16/03/2023	25	3:16 AM
17/03/2023	26	4:28 AM	17/03/2023	26	4:03 AM
18/03/2023	27	5:12 AM	18/03/2023	27	4:41 AM
19/03/2023	28	5:50 AM	19/03/2023	28	5:10 AM
20/03/2023	29	6:23 AM	20/03/2023	29	5:35 AM
21/03/2023	30	6:54 AM	21/03/2023	30	5:57 AM
21/03/2023	1	1:26 PM	21/03/2023	1	5:26 PM
22/03/2023	2	7:24 AM	22/03/2023	2	6:17 AM
23/03/2023	3	7:55 AM	23/03/2023	3	6:38 AM
24/03/2023	4	8:27 AM	24/03/2023	4	7:01 AM
25/03/2023	5	9:03 AM	25/03/2023	5	7:28 AM
26/03/2023	6	9:43 AM	26/03/2023	6	9:00 AM
27/03/2023	7	10:27 AM	27/03/2023	7	9:38 AM
28/03/2023	8	11:16 AM	28/03/2023	8	10:25 AM
29/03/2023	9	12:10 PM	29/03/2023	9	11:19 AM
30/03/2023	10	1:07 PM	30/03/2023	10	12:19 PM
31/03/2023	11	2:05 PM	31/03/2023	11	1:24 PM

You can find the description of each lunar day in the chapter "A Guide to The Moon Cycle and Lunar Days"

March is usually not a very good month for you – but this year is an exception! The stars are aligned, and Venus and Jupiter are both in your sign – hat could be better?

Work. For the most part, March is a time for relaxing, making family-related decisions, and romance. However, if you are an incurable workaholic and, in your world, work comes first, you will still be able to accomplish a lot for your own business, even during this fairly lazy month.

The best time for any work-related events is the first or last 10 days of the month, when you will be able to make decent money, hold necessary meetings, and surround yourself with like-minded individuals, or simply the right people.

During the second 10 days of March, things are not so rosy. During this time, you might receive unpleasant news from a colleague from another city or abroad, and it may involve gossip or outright deceit.

During this time, much of what your partners or opponents would like to keep under the table might come to light, and you will find yourself dealing with it during the last 10 days of the month, which promise to be more favorable. However, you are in a strong position – in the end, you will achieve clarity and assert your own rules in the game of life.

Employees might also face trouble at work. During the middle of the month, you are likely to face unexpected audits, which will throw a wrench in your usual working process. However, everything will turn out just fine, as the last 10 days of March are expected to be a quiet, calm time.

Any business travel should be planned for the first 20 days of the month.

Money. Financially, March is a very favorable time for you. You will have regular income, and you might receive some unexpected surprises, too. This is especially the case for the first and last 10 days of the month.

Love and family . March is a very positive time for your personal life, as well. It is the perfect time for relaxing with your family, relatives, and loved ones. You might plan a trip for a week or two to get away from work, gain new perspective, and restore your body and soul.

This is also a great time for single people – your chances of meeting your soulmate are very high this month! Your time has come!

Your relationship with relatives may grow more complicated once again, and that is most likely during the second 10 days of the month, when some family members' secrets suddenly emerge. Later on, however, you will be able to smooth things over thanks to your own efforts.

Any leisure travel should be planned for the first or last 10 days of the month. If your plans overlap with the second, more difficult 10 days of March, be careful with your documents and try to avoid any jaunts to difficult, dangerous destinations.

Health. As usual, your energy is lagging in March. If you take care to lead a healthy lifestyle, however, there is no reason to fear.

March is also the ideal time for any cosmetic procedures or plastic surgery.

During the second 10 days of the month, take extra care when traveling or driving.

April

New York Time			London Time		
Calendar Day	Lunar Day	Lunar Day Start Time	Calendar Day	Lunar Day	Lunar Day Start Time
01/04/2023	12	3:04 PM	01/04/2023	12	2:30 PM
02/04/2023	13	4:04 PM	02/04/2023	13	3:38 PM
03/04/2023	14	5:04 PM	03/04/2023	14	4:46 PM
04/04/2023	15	6:05 PM	04/04/2023	15	5:56 PM
05/04/2023	16	7:07 PM	05/04/2023	16	7:06 PM
06/04/2023	17	8:11 PM	06/04/2023	17	8:18 PM
07/04/2023	18	9:16 PM	07/04/2023	18	9:32 PM
08/04/2023	19	10:23 PM	08/04/2023	19	10:47 PM
09/04/2023	20	11:30 PM	10/04/2023	20	12:02 AM
11/04/2023	21	12:34 AM	11/04/2023	21	1:11 AM
12/04/2023	22	1:33 AM	12/04/2023	22	2:12 AM
13/04/2023	23	2:25 AM	13/04/2023	23	3:02 AM
14/04/2023	24	3:10 AM	14/04/2023	24	3:41 AM
15/04/2023	25	3:48 AM	15/04/2023	25	4:12 AM
16/04/2023	26	4:22 AM	16/04/2023	26	4:38 AM
17/04/2023	27	4:53 AM	17/04/2023	27	5:00 AM
18/04/2023	28	5:22 AM	18/04/2023	28	5:20 AM
19/04/2023	29	5:52 AM	19/04/2023	29	5:40 AM
20/04/2023	1	12:15 AM	20/04/2023	1	5:15 AM
20/04/2023	2	6:23 AM	20/04/2023	2	6:02 AM
21/04/2023	3	6:57 AM	21/04/2023	3	6:27 AM
22/04/2023	4	7:35 AM	22/04/2023	4	6:56 AM
23/04/2023	5	8:18 AM	23/04/2023	5	7:32 AM
24/04/2023	6	9:06 AM	24/04/2023	6	8:15 AM
25/04/2023	7	9:59 AM	25/04/2023	7	9:07 AM
26/04/2023	8	10:55 AM	26/04/2023	8	10:06 AM
27/04/2023	9	11:53 AM	27/04/2023	9	11:09 AM
28/04/2023	10	12:52 PM	28/04/2023	10	12:15 PM
29/04/2023	11	1:52 PM	29/04/2023	11	1:23 PM
30/04/2023	12	2:51 PM	30/04/2023	12	2:30 PM

You can find the description of each lunar day in the chapter "A Guide to The Moon Cycle and Lunar Days"

This month, you will not be defending your boundaries so much as expanding them. And everything will work out for you!

Work. April is one of the best months of the year, when the planets come together and bring many opportunities. That may mean renewing old ties and making new acquaintances that are incredibly useful to your business development. You will discuss your projects with new business partners and old colleagues, and most importantly, find the money you need to make this happen. This applies to business owners or managers at any level.

Employees can count on support from management – right now, you are able to come to your bosses with any request or suggestion, and they will most likely allow you to convince them. Overall, roll up your sleeves and get to work, and you will not have to wait long for success.

Money. Financially, April is a great time for you. Your achievements this month may have a major effect on your wallet in both April and May. Nearly all Aries can count on significantly higher income, whether from your usual salary or unofficial sources.

That may include profits from various real estate transactions, credit, or support from loved ones. This month, you are so lucky with money that any efforts you put into this direction are sure to lead to success.

Love and family. Those focused on their personal lives may be busy improving your home this month. That could be construction, repairs, or other efforts that will continue, and you can expect help on all fronts, here.

Couples might look toward the past and reconsider their relationships. If you recently had a quarrel, this month, you will manage to overcome it all, reach an understanding, and a path toward reconciliation. But if you are feeling any shreds of guilt, apologize, and you can expect a positive reaction from your partner.

Those with problems involving their children will also have a good opportunity this month to smooth things over. This is a great time for making amends!

Health. In April, you will feel a strong surge of energy, despite the heavy workload, and you will feel better than ever. Naturally, you have no reason to fear falling ill.

May

New York Time			London Time		
Calendar Day	Lunar Day	Lunar Day Start Time	Calendar Day	Lunar Day	Lunar Day Start Time
01/05/2023	13	3:52 PM	01/05/2023	13	3:39 PM
02/05/2023	14	4:53 PM	02/05/2023	14	4:48 PM
03/05/2023	15	5:56 PM	03/05/2023	15	6:00 PM
04/05/2023	16	7:02 PM	04/05/2023	16	7:14 PM
05/05/2023	17	8:09 PM	05/05/2023	17	8:30 PM
06/05/2023	18	9:18 PM	06/05/2023	18	9:47 PM
07/05/2023	19	10:25 PM	07/05/2023	19	11:00 PM
08/05/2023	20	11:27 PM	09/05/2023	20	12:06 AM
10/05/2023	21	12:22 AM	10/05/2023	21	1:01 AM
11/05/2023	22	1:10 AM	11/05/2023	22	1:43 AM
12/05/2023	23	1:50 AM	12/05/2023	23	2:16 AM
13/05/2023	24	2:24 AM	13/05/2023	24	2:43 AM
14/05/2023	25	2:55 AM	14/05/2023	25	3:05 AM
15/05/2023	26	3:24 AM	15/05/2023	26	3:25 AM
16/05/2023	27	3:53 AM	16/05/2023	27	3:45 AM
17/05/2023	28	4:23 AM	17/05/2023	28	4:05 AM
18/05/2023	29	4:55 AM	18/05/2023	29	4:28 AM
19/05/2023	30	5:31 AM	19/05/2023	30	4:55 AM
19/05/2023	1	11:55 AM	19/05/2023	1	4:55 PM
20/05/2023	2	6:11 AM	20/05/2023	2	5:27 AM
21/05/2023	3	6:57 AM	21/05/2023	3	6:08 AM
22/05/2023	4	7:48 AM	22/05/2023	4	6:56 AM
23/05/2023	5	8:44 AM	23/05/2023	5	7:53 AM
24/05/2023	6	9:42 AM	24/05/2023	6	8:55 AM
25/05/2023	7	10:41 AM	25/05/2023	7	10:01 AM
26/05/2023	8	11:40 AM	26/05/2023	8	11:07 AM
27/05/2023	9	12:39 PM	27/05/2023	9	12:14 PM
28/05/2023	10	1:38 PM	28/05/2023	10	1:22 PM
29/05/2023	11	2:38 PM	29/05/2023	11	2:30 PM
30/05/2023	12	3:39 PM	30/05/2023	12	3:40 PM
31/05/2023	13	4:43 PM	31/05/2023	13	4:52 PM

You can find the description of each lunar day in the chapter "A Guide to The Moon Cycle and Lunar Days"

May bring flowers and new beginnings alike. This month, keep in mind that the more quietly you move, the further you will go.

Work. During the first half of the month, things will move slowly, but it is also a time of great responsibility.

This is most likely related to accounting or distributing finances. You may negotiate with partners regarding major financial or administrative matters, as well.

Until May 15, Mercury will be in retrograde, which means that you may experience difficulties and setbacks. The stars recommend being cautious, responsible, and never rushing things.

In the end, everything will go as planned, and the delays will allow you to correct any errors and ensure that you are meticulous as you can be.

Employees might raise the issue of a raise, bonus, or benefits, and following some discussions, your wishes will be granted.

Many will continue to expand their business, and a significant part of your expenses will include work-related purchases, as well as various real estate transactions. You may need to get a loan or otherwise obtain funding for this purpose.

Money. This month, your finances are doing well. You will have a regular income, in addition to some profits from work you completed in earlier months, or perhaps a bonus or favorable credit.

Expect the greatest sums to come in on May 1, 2, 9-11, 18, 19, 28, 29.

Love and family. If your personal life comes first, you may find yourself immersed in a variety of household tasks. Many will be busy setting up their living space, which will occupy a lot of your family's resources or those of a relative. It is likely you will be able to cover these costs on your own, however.

Your relationship with your family is harmonious, and noticeably better these days.

Many Aries will take some time off from work in early May and perhaps travel, relax, and maybe even engage in some important business networking.

Mercury will be in retrograde until May 15, and this is a good time to renew old ties, meet up with former classmates, friends, and acquaintances you may have fallen out of touch with for various reasons.

Though you may meet new people during this period, they are unlikely to be reliable. Expect them to make a swift exit from their life, leaving nothing but less-than pleasant memories.

Health. This month, you are feeling somewhat sluggish, but it won't get worse than that. You can engage in self–care – perhaps a massage, a trip to the cosmetologist, or simply relaxing with a good book on a soft couch. The first half of May is the best time for any of this.

June

New York Time				London Time		
Calendar Day	Lunar Day	Lunar Day Start Time		Calendar Day	Lunar Day	Lunar Day Start Time
01/06/2023	14	5:50 PM		01/06/2023	14	6:07 PM
02/06/2023	15	6:59 PM		02/06/2023	15	7:24 PM
03/06/2023	16	8:08 PM		03/06/2023	16	8:41 PM
04/06/2023	17	9:14 PM		04/06/2023	17	9:52 PM
05/06/2023	18	10:14 PM		05/06/2023	18	10:53 PM
06/06/2023	19	11:06 PM		06/06/2023	19	11:41 PM
07/06/2023	20	11:50 PM		08/06/2023	20	12:19 AM
09/06/2023	21	12:27 AM		09/06/2023	21	12:48 AM
10/06/2023	22	12:59 AM		10/06/2023	22	1:11 AM
11/06/2023	23	1:29 AM		11/06/2023	23	1:32 AM
12/06/2023	24	1:57 AM		12/06/2023	24	1:52 AM
13/06/2023	25	2:26 AM		13/06/2023	25	2:11 AM
14/06/2023	26	2:56 AM		14/06/2023	26	2:33 AM
15/06/2023	27	3:30 AM		15/06/2023	27	2:57 AM
16/06/2023	28	4:08 AM		16/06/2023	28	3:27 AM
17/06/2023	29	4:51 AM		17/06/2023	29	4:04 AM
18/06/2023	1	12:39 AM		18/06/2023	30	4:49 AM
18/06/2023	2	5:40 AM		18/06/2023	1	5:39 AM
19/06/2023	3	6:34 AM		19/06/2023	2	5:42 AM
20/06/2023	4	7:31 AM		20/06/2023	3	6:43 AM
21/06/2023	5	8:30 AM		21/06/2023	4	7:47 AM
22/06/2023	6	9:29 AM		22/06/2023	5	8:54 AM
23/06/2023	7	10:28 AM		23/06/2023	6	10:01 AM
24/06/2023	8	11:27 AM		24/06/2023	7	11:07 AM
25/06/2023	9	12:25 PM		25/06/2023	8	12:14 PM
26/06/2023	10	1:25 PM		26/06/2023	9	1:22 PM
27/06/2023	11	2:27 PM		27/06/2023	10	2:32 PM
28/06/2023	12	3:31 PM		28/06/2023	11	3:44 PM
29/06/2023	13	4:37 PM		29/06/2023	12	4:59 PM
30/06/2023	14	5:46 PM		30/06/2023	13	6:15 PM

You can find the description of each lunar day in the chapter "A Guide to The Moon Cycle and Lunar Days"

June will bring you a surge of energy, along with the wisdom to use it where you need it most. With this in your arsenal, you can move mountains!

Work. June is not a time to sit back and relax for most Aries. You are in touch with colleagues in other cities or abroad, and you might take a successful trip. But not everything with your faraway partners is going smoothly. You may face challenges that have roots in the past and have unexpectedly reared their heads once again. This time, however, you will overcome things more quickly. Let the past remain in the past, and you are sure to reach a mutually beneficial partnership.

Many Aries, especially business owners and upper-level managers, will have to deal with important day-to-day matters this month. Things will run smoothly, and you will avoid any setbacks or trouble.

Employees will have a great opportunity to increase their income. That may be a promotion that includes a higher salary, or perhaps a job at a new, more promising organization.

Money. June is a great time for your wallet. Many Aries will be pleased to see a higher income, and that is likely to remain the case in the future.

Expect the largest sums to come in on June 5, 6, 14, 15, and 23-25.

There are always expenses, and most of them will be related to leisure, your children, and loved ones this month.

Love and family. There are changes underfoot in your personal life. Your relationship with relatives is growing closer, and you might travel together or meet with family members living in other cities or abroad. If you have any old grudges, they will be smoothed over.

Your children are a source of joy but expect to spend a large share of the family budget resolving their problems during the second half of the month.

Couples may swing from one extreme to another. Unexpectedly, you will discover that your viewpoints clash on certain subjects. Issues over your shared finances and other material issues or different value systems will come as a surprise. You may find yourself arguing all month long, but there is hope that you will get through it.

The stars recommend that you don't get greedy or ask for too much if you want to keep the problem small. What's more, you had money before, you still have it, and it is not going anywhere in the future.

Single people and those who have been disappointed by past relationships can count on meeting someone new and a torrid romance. Whether things pan out depends on your plans and intentions, but there is a chance your relationship might continue.

Health. In June, you are feeling energetic and have no reason to fear falling ill.

Be especially careful when driving and traveling from June 15 to 18.

July

<table>
<tr><th colspan="3">New York Time</th><th colspan="3">London Time</th></tr>
<tr><th>Calendar Day</th><th>Lunar Day</th><th>Lunar Day Start Time</th><th>Calendar Day</th><th>Lunar Day</th><th>Lunar Day Start Time</th></tr>
<tr><td>01/07/2023</td><td>15</td><td>6:54 PM</td><td>01/07/2023</td><td>14</td><td>7:30 PM</td></tr>
<tr><td>02/07/2023</td><td>16</td><td>7:58 PM</td><td>02/07/2023</td><td>15</td><td>8:37 PM</td></tr>
<tr><td>03/07/2023</td><td>17</td><td>8:55 PM</td><td>03/07/2023</td><td>16</td><td>9:33 PM</td></tr>
<tr><td>04/07/2023</td><td>18</td><td>9:44 PM</td><td>04/07/2023</td><td>17</td><td>10:16 PM</td></tr>
<tr><td>05/07/2023</td><td>19</td><td>10:25 PM</td><td>05/07/2023</td><td>18</td><td>10:49 PM</td></tr>
<tr><td>06/07/2023</td><td>20</td><td>11:00 PM</td><td>06/07/2023</td><td>19</td><td>11:15 PM</td></tr>
<tr><td>07/07/2023</td><td>21</td><td>11:31 PM</td><td>07/07/2023</td><td>20</td><td>11:38 PM</td></tr>
<tr><td>09/07/2023</td><td>22</td><td>12:01 AM</td><td>08/07/2023</td><td>21</td><td>11:58 PM</td></tr>
<tr><td>10/07/2023</td><td>23</td><td>12:29 AM</td><td>10/07/2023</td><td>22</td><td>12:18 AM</td></tr>
<tr><td>11/07/2023</td><td>24</td><td>12:59 AM</td><td>11/07/2023</td><td>23</td><td>12:39 AM</td></tr>
<tr><td>12/07/2023</td><td>25</td><td>1:32 AM</td><td>12/07/2023</td><td>24</td><td>1:02 AM</td></tr>
<tr><td>13/07/2023</td><td>26</td><td>2:08 AM</td><td>13/07/2023</td><td>25</td><td>1:30 AM</td></tr>
<tr><td>14/07/2023</td><td>27</td><td>2:49 AM</td><td>14/07/2023</td><td>26</td><td>2:04 AM</td></tr>
<tr><td>15/07/2023</td><td>28</td><td>3:36 AM</td><td>15/07/2023</td><td>27</td><td>2:46 AM</td></tr>
<tr><td>16/07/2023</td><td>29</td><td>4:28 AM</td><td>16/07/2023</td><td>28</td><td>3:36 AM</td></tr>
<tr><td>17/07/2023</td><td>30</td><td>5:24 AM</td><td>17/07/2023</td><td>29</td><td>4:34 AM</td></tr>
<tr><td>17/07/2023</td><td>1</td><td>2:33 PM</td><td>17/07/2023</td><td>1</td><td>7:33 PM</td></tr>
<tr><td>18/07/2023</td><td>2</td><td>6:22 AM</td><td>18/07/2023</td><td>2</td><td>5:37 AM</td></tr>
<tr><td>19/07/2023</td><td>3</td><td>7:21 AM</td><td>19/07/2023</td><td>3</td><td>6:43 AM</td></tr>
<tr><td>20/07/2023</td><td>4</td><td>8:20 AM</td><td>20/07/2023</td><td>4</td><td>7:50 AM</td></tr>
<tr><td>21/07/2023</td><td>5</td><td>9:19 AM</td><td>21/07/2023</td><td>5</td><td>8:56 AM</td></tr>
<tr><td>22/07/2023</td><td>6</td><td>10:17 AM</td><td>22/07/2023</td><td>6</td><td>10:03 AM</td></tr>
<tr><td>23/07/2023</td><td>7</td><td>11:15 AM</td><td>23/07/2023</td><td>7</td><td>11:09 AM</td></tr>
<tr><td>24/07/2023</td><td>8</td><td>12:15 PM</td><td>24/07/2023</td><td>8</td><td>12:17 PM</td></tr>
<tr><td>25/07/2023</td><td>9</td><td>1:16 PM</td><td>25/07/2023</td><td>9</td><td>1:27 PM</td></tr>
<tr><td>26/07/2023</td><td>10</td><td>2:20 PM</td><td>26/07/2023</td><td>10</td><td>2:39 PM</td></tr>
<tr><td>27/07/2023</td><td>11</td><td>3:26 PM</td><td>27/07/2023</td><td>11</td><td>3:53 PM</td></tr>
<tr><td>28/07/2023</td><td>12</td><td>4:33 PM</td><td>28/07/2023</td><td>12</td><td>5:07 PM</td></tr>
<tr><td>29/07/2023</td><td>13</td><td>5:39 PM</td><td>29/07/2023</td><td>13</td><td>6:16 PM</td></tr>
<tr><td>30/07/2023</td><td>14</td><td>6:39 PM</td><td>30/07/2023</td><td>14</td><td>7:17 PM</td></tr>
<tr><td>31/07/2023</td><td>15</td><td>7:32 PM</td><td>31/07/2023</td><td>15</td><td>8:07 PM</td></tr>
</table>

You can find the description of each lunar day in the chapter "A Guide to The Moon Cycle and Lunar Days"

This month, you will have to juggle several projects at the same time. You will also have to choose between leisure and working on your tan and busying yourself with hard work on the household front.

Work. Incurable workaholics – and they are well-represented among Aries – will spend much of July on everyday and administrative tasks. You are likely to continue with major construction, repairs, and many bothersome jobs related to this.

Business owners and managers at every level are advised to be careful with their subordinates – their mistakes may cost you dearly. The last 10 days of July will be the most indicative here, when a colleague's shortcomings will cause unexpected problems. You may also see intrigue from secret enemies and competitors during this period.

Employees will spend most of the month busy with family matters, but during the last 10 days of the month, and you will have to deal with problems on your team stemming from gossipy colleagues. Someone in your circle may bring to light information that you would have rather kept secret.

From July first to 19, things will be quieter. Any events planned during this period will go as expected, without any holdups or problems.

Money. July is a great time for your finances. You will have steady income, and significantly more of it. Expect the largest sums to come in on July 3, 4, 7, 11-14, 30, and 31.

Your expenses are pleasant in July – shopping, relaxation, your children's needs – not only can you afford it all, but it's the best investment in your personal life.

Love and family. Those who are not part of the working world may be busy with their personal lives this month. You are working on improving your household and various tasks related to real estate. This pleasant summer month is a great time for relaxation, which is best planned with your family, relatives, and loved ones.

Some Aries will head somewhere faraway, while others will go to a summer house or visit relatives who live nearby.

Families will be harmonious, and many Aries will be busy with their children's affairs and spend a lot on their unexpected needs.

This month will bring pleasant surprises to couples, as well as unexpected irritation. The stars recommend not being stingy or making any demands of your partner in order to avoid any disagreements.

Health. The elderly or those with chronic diseases should be especially careful during the last 10 days of July. Illnesses may creep up unexpectedly and cause a lot of anxiety during this time.

August

New York Time			London Time		
Calendar Day	Lunar Day	Lunar Day Start Time	Calendar Day	Lunar Day	Lunar Day Start Time
01/08/2023	16	8:17 PM	01/08/2023	16	8:45 PM
02/08/2023	17	8:56 PM	02/08/2023	17	9:15 PM
03/08/2023	18	9:30 PM	03/08/2023	18	9:40 PM
04/08/2023	19	10:01 PM	04/08/2023	19	10:02 PM
05/08/2023	20	10:31 PM	05/08/2023	20	10:22 PM
06/08/2023	21	11:01 PM	06/08/2023	21	10:44 PM
07/08/2023	22	11:33 PM	07/08/2023	22	11:07 PM
09/08/2023	23	12:09 AM	08/08/2023	23	11:33 PM
10/08/2023	24	12:49 AM	10/08/2023	24	12:05 AM
11/08/2023	25	1:34 AM	11/08/2023	25	12:44 AM
12/08/2023	26	2:24 AM	12/08/2023	26	1:32 AM
13/08/2023	27	3:18 AM	13/08/2023	27	2:27 AM
14/08/2023	28	4:16 AM	14/08/2023	28	3:29 AM
15/08/2023	29	5:14 AM	15/08/2023	29	4:34 AM
16/08/2023	1	5:38 AM	15/08/2023	30	5:41 AM
16/08/2023	2	6:13 AM	16/08/2023	1	10:38 AM
17/08/2023	3	7:12 AM	17/08/2023	2	6:47 AM
18/08/2023	4	8:10 AM	18/08/2023	3	7:54 AM
19/08/2023	5	9:09 AM	19/08/2023	4	9:00 AM
20/08/2023	6	10:08 AM	20/08/2023	5	10:07 AM
21/08/2023	7	11:08 AM	21/08/2023	6	11:16 AM
22/08/2023	8	12:10 PM	22/08/2023	7	12:25 PM
23/08/2023	9	1:13 PM	23/08/2023	8	1:37 PM
24/08/2023	10	2:18 PM	24/08/2023	9	2:49 PM
25/08/2023	11	3:22 PM	25/08/2023	10	3:59 PM
26/08/2023	12	4:23 PM	26/08/2023	11	5:02 PM
27/08/2023	13	5:18 PM	27/08/2023	12	5:56 PM
28/08/2023	14	6:06 PM	28/08/2023	13	6:38 PM
29/08/2023	15	6:48 PM	29/08/2023	14	7:12 PM
30/08/2023	16	7:24 PM	30/08/2023	15	7:39 PM
31/08/2023	17	7:57 PM	31/08/2023	16	8:03 PM

You can find the description of each lunar day in the chapter "A Guide to The Moon Cycle and Lunar Days"

August is a fantastic month for you! Expect to spend this month simultaneously relaxing in nature while also striving for the good of your business or family.

Work. In August, you will be proving the wonders of stamina and perseverance. Most Aries will rely on these qualities to combine things they would have never imagined before – work and relaxation.

That will look differently in each specific case, and generally speaking, it is impossible to predict, but the stars will give you an incredible opportunity here.

Managers and business owners can count on their subordinates but remember – trust but verify still applies! The last 10 days of August will be most telling, when errors by your team or other colleagues might become particularly noticeable. All month long, remember to keep your finger on the pulse of the goings-on, and give them the direction they need.

During the last 10 days of August, employees should be extra careful when reviewing documents, especially if they are financial in nature, and avoid slacking off at work. Remember – avoid trying to make any shortcuts!

Money. Financially speaking, August might look uneven. Money will be coming in regularly, and there will be significantly more of it than usual. But you will also have higher expenses. Vacation, travel, children, and your loved ones all require funds. This is a great month for you, however, so you won't find yourself in ruins, because your higher income makes up for the spending.

Love and family. August is a fantastic summer month, and for most of it, you will be focused on relaxation, relatives, and loved ones. A change of scenery and investing in yourself are both wise and the right step, right now.

However, it is not worth aiming for a new, unknown location. Head to a place you have been several times in the past. Venus is in retrograde in the sector of the sky related to relaxation, adventure, and entertainment. New places might not live up to your expectations, and you will find yourself disappointed.

Your relationship with your family is overall harmonious, but you may have some hiccups with your children, who will incur major expenses. If that is the case, try to separate needs from wants and carefully examine your children's demands.

August is a difficult time for unmarried couples. Romantically inclined Aries will have to contend with the complex nature of love. Feelings may be fickle, and suddenly disappear when you least expect it, only to resurrect once again.

Right now, any time you want to say "yes" or "no", your heart will start pulling you in the other direction. The stars recommend that you sit down and really get in touch with your feelings, avoid jumping to any hasty conclusions, and in general try to be less anxious and nervous.

Health. In August, you will be full of energy and have no reason to fear falling ill. You may be a bit confrontational by nature, but right now, take off your armor, lay down your sword, and find some time to relax. The stars recommend visiting the spa, getting a massage, taking a trip to the sea, or just a long walk in nature.

September

New York Time				London Time		
Calendar Day	Lunar Day	Lunar Day Start Time		Calendar Day	Lunar Day	Lunar Day Start Time
01/09/2023	18	8:28 PM		01/09/2023	17	8:24 PM
02/09/2023	19	8:59 PM		02/09/2023	18	8:46 PM
03/09/2023	20	9:32 PM		03/09/2023	19	9:09 PM
04/09/2023	21	10:07 PM		04/09/2023	20	9:34 PM
05/09/2023	22	10:46 PM		05/09/2023	21	10:05 PM
06/09/2023	23	11:30 PM		06/09/2023	22	10:43 PM
08/09/2023	24	12:19 AM		07/09/2023	23	11:28 PM
09/09/2023	25	1:13 AM		09/09/2023	24	12:21 AM
10/09/2023	26	2:09 AM		10/09/2023	25	1:21 AM
11/09/2023	27	3:08 AM		11/09/2023	26	2:25 AM
12/09/2023	28	4:07 AM		12/09/2023	27	3:31 AM
13/09/2023	29	5:05 AM		13/09/2023	28	4:38 AM
14/09/2023	30	6:04 AM		14/09/2023	29	5:45 AM
14/09/2023	1	9:40 PM		15/09/2023	1	2:40 AM
15/09/2023	2	7:03 AM		15/09/2023	2	6:52 AM
16/09/2023	3	8:02 AM		16/09/2023	3	7:59 AM
17/09/2023	4	9:02 AM		17/09/2023	4	9:07 AM
18/09/2023	5	10:03 AM		18/09/2023	5	10:16 AM
19/09/2023	6	11:06 AM		19/09/2023	6	11:27 AM
20/09/2023	7	12:10 PM		20/09/2023	7	12:39 PM
21/09/2023	8	1:13 PM		21/09/2023	8	1:48 PM
22/09/2023	9	2:13 PM		22/09/2023	9	2:52 PM
23/09/2023	10	3:09 PM		23/09/2023	10	3:48 PM
24/09/2023	11	3:58 PM		24/09/2023	11	4:33 PM
25/09/2023	12	4:41 PM		25/09/2023	12	5:09 PM
26/09/2023	13	5:18 PM		26/09/2023	13	5:38 PM
27/09/2023	14	5:52 PM		27/09/2023	14	6:03 PM
28/09/2023	15	6:24 PM		28/09/2023	15	6:25 PM
29/09/2023	16	6:55 PM		29/09/2023	16	6:46 PM
30/09/2023	17	7:27 PM		30/09/2023	17	7:08 PM

You can find the description of each lunar day in the chapter "A Guide to The Moon Cycle and Lunar Days"

You are an active, detail-oriented perfectionist, and it's hard for you to tolerate anything holding back your ideas. The most important thing is that you are on the right track, and in the end, everything will work out!

Work. September is a rush of activity, and you have a lot of work to do. You are striving toward your goals, but not everything is turning out the way you had imagined. Any events you plan will develop at a snail's pace, and you will constantly have to come back to the same issues and adjust your plans and activities.

Business owners and managers are advised to keep a closer eye on their subordinates, especially when it comes to financial matters. Remember that not everyone on your team might be responsible and honest, so keep your finger on the pulse of what's going on.

Employees may encounter disagreements, rumors, gossip, and arguments on their team. The stars recommend that you keep your head down and put your nose to the grindstone. Pay no mind to the pettiness around you, which might just be making mountains out of molehills, anyway. This situation will be over soon, anyway. By the second half of the month, everything will be back in order.

During the first half of September, the stars recommend meticulously checking any information and reading over any documents. Mercury will be in retrograde until September 15, and that often means misunderstandings and errors.

Money. Despite the problems at work, your pocketbook is just fine. You will have regular income, and somewhat more of it, too. Expect the largest sums to come in on September 4, 5, 13-15, 20, 23, 24, and 30.

Your expenses are low and most of them are related to your children or loved ones.

Love and family. Your personal life has been on the back burner, as most of the important events this month are taking place at work. But you can't totally ignore love or family, as they are the most important things in your life and taking care of your children involves spending money, too. This is probably not news to you.

September is a hard time for couples. Problems from the past have appeared once again, but this time, things look much simpler. Remember that even a tiny step toward compromise will go a long way to simmering down the tension. Closer to the end of the month, you will find your passion again, and everything will be harmonious.

Health. In September, you will feel a bit run-down if you are elderly or weakened. You are advised to take care of yourself and turn to your doctor for help whenever you need it.

Those who are young and strong should lead a healthy lifestyle.

September is a great time to end bad habits, visit a cosmetologist, and engage in some more intensive self-care routines.

October

New York Time			London Time		
Calendar Day	Lunar Day	Lunar Day Start Time	Calendar Day	Lunar Day	Lunar Day Start Time
01/10/2023	18	8:02 PM	01/10/2023	18	7:33 PM
02/10/2023	19	8:40 PM	02/10/2023	19	8:02 PM
03/10/2023	20	9:23 PM	03/10/2023	20	8:38 PM
04/10/2023	21	10:11 PM	04/10/2023	21	9:21 PM
05/10/2023	22	11:04 PM	05/10/2023	22	10:12 PM
07/10/2023	23	12:01 AM	06/10/2023	23	11:11 PM
08/10/2023	24	12:59 AM	08/10/2023	24	12:14 AM
09/10/2023	25	1:58 AM	09/10/2023	25	1:20 AM
10/10/2023	26	2:57 AM	10/10/2023	26	2:27 AM
11/10/2023	27	3:56 AM	11/10/2023	27	3:34 AM
12/10/2023	28	4:54 AM	12/10/2023	28	4:40 AM
13/10/2023	29	5:54 AM	13/10/2023	29	5:48 AM
14/10/2023	30	6:54 AM	14/10/2023	30	6:56 AM
14/10/2023	1	1:55 PM	14/10/2023	1	6:55 PM
15/10/2023	2	7:55 AM	15/10/2023	2	8:06 AM
16/10/2023	3	8:59 AM	16/10/2023	3	9:17 AM
17/10/2023	4	10:03 AM	17/10/2023	4	10:29 AM
18/10/2023	5	11:07 AM	18/10/2023	5	11:40 AM
19/10/2023	6	12:08 PM	19/10/2023	6	12:46 PM
20/10/2023	7	1:05 PM	20/10/2023	7	1:44 PM
21/10/2023	8	1:55 PM	21/10/2023	8	2:32 PM
22/10/2023	9	2:38 PM	22/10/2023	9	3:09 PM
23/10/2023	10	3:16 PM	23/10/2023	10	3:40 PM
24/10/2023	11	3:50 PM	24/10/2023	11	4:05 PM
25/10/2023	12	4:21 PM	25/10/2023	12	4:27 PM
26/10/2023	13	4:51 PM	26/10/2023	13	4:48 PM
27/10/2023	14	5:22 PM	27/10/2023	14	5:09 PM
28/10/2023	15	5:55 PM	28/10/2023	15	5:32 PM
29/10/2023	16	6:32 PM	29/10/2023	16	4:59 PM
30/10/2023	17	7:13 PM	30/10/2023	17	5:31 PM
31/10/2023	18	8:00 PM	31/10/2023	18	6:11 PM

You can find the description of each lunar day in the chapter "A Guide to The Moon Cycle and Lunar Days"

October's two eclipses will remind you of the importance of working together. Remember, no man is an island, and that is very valid advice for you right now.

Work. The most important thing this month is your relationship with business partners, and right now, your professional success depends on your ability to make that connection. There is no point in trying to have the last word right now, and flexibility and diplomacy are what you need.

The topic of the day is probably money or something of material value, and you will be immersed in discussions over this, whether you are a business owner or a manager of any level. The astrologist predicts that you will have the upper hand, which you should appreciate as you consider your partners' positions.

What's more, remember that bad peace is better than a good war, so avoid any arguments and do whatever needs to be done intentionally and diplomatically.

You can expect a lot of support from your colleagues and subordinates. Despite the minor inconsistencies at work, their efforts will be positive.

Employees will encounter some opposition from competitors, and the stars recommend watching your back. Your troubles will not be serious, however, and will be contained to gossip and minor intrigue.

Money. Financially, October is a great time for you. You will have regular income and much more of it than usual. Expect the largest sums to come in on October 1, 2, 11, 12, 20, 21, 29 and 30.

Your expenses are growing, however. The last 10 days of October are when you will spend the most, especially from October 28-30. That may be related to work, or perhaps your personal needs.

Love and family. If your personal life is most important to you, here, the stars recommend that you keep an eye on your loved ones. Otherwise, you may end up hurting those around you and later come to regret it. You might expect an argument over the family budget, and here, your spouse's position may vary. You will win out in the end, so it is not worth piling too hard on your better half. Try to resolve delicate issues peacefully. Your loved ones will appreciate it, and a little later they will thank you.

In many families, you are going to need a lot of money to improve an old home, or perhaps buy a new one. As you know, that is a lot of work, and it doesn't come cheap.

Health. In October, you are not feeling particularly energetic, and that will be most noticeable during the last 10 days of the month. Take care of yourself during this time and try to avoid any fall colds or infections. Don't push yourself too hard. This is especially relevant during the eclipse on October 28-30.

November

<table>
<tr><td colspan="3" align="center">New York Time</td><td colspan="3" align="center">London Time</td></tr>
<tr><td align="center">Calendar
Day</td><td align="center">Lunar
Day</td><td align="center">Lunar Day
Start Time</td><td align="center">Calendar
Day</td><td align="center">Lunar
Day</td><td align="center">Lunar Day
Start Time</td></tr>
<tr><td>01/11/2023</td><td>19</td><td>8:52 PM</td><td>01/11/2023</td><td>19</td><td>7:00 PM</td></tr>
<tr><td>02/11/2023</td><td>20</td><td>9:49 PM</td><td>02/11/2023</td><td>20</td><td>7:57 PM</td></tr>
<tr><td>03/11/2023</td><td>21</td><td>10:47 PM</td><td>03/11/2023</td><td>21</td><td>9:00 PM</td></tr>
<tr><td>04/11/2023</td><td>22</td><td>11:47 PM</td><td>04/11/2023</td><td>22</td><td>10:06 PM</td></tr>
<tr><td>05/11/2023</td><td>23</td><td>11:46 PM</td><td>05/11/2023</td><td>23</td><td>11:13 PM</td></tr>
<tr><td>07/11/2023</td><td>24</td><td>12:45 AM</td><td>07/11/2023</td><td>24</td><td>12:20 AM</td></tr>
<tr><td>08/11/2023</td><td>25</td><td>1:43 AM</td><td>08/11/2023</td><td>25</td><td>1:26 AM</td></tr>
<tr><td>09/11/2023</td><td>26</td><td>2:42 AM</td><td>09/11/2023</td><td>26</td><td>2:33 AM</td></tr>
<tr><td>10/11/2023</td><td>27</td><td>3:42 AM</td><td>10/11/2023</td><td>27</td><td>3:41 AM</td></tr>
<tr><td>11/11/2023</td><td>28</td><td>4:43 AM</td><td>11/11/2023</td><td>28</td><td>4:50 AM</td></tr>
<tr><td>12/11/2023</td><td>29</td><td>5:46 AM</td><td>12/11/2023</td><td>29</td><td>6:02 AM</td></tr>
<tr><td>13/11/2023</td><td>1</td><td>4:27 AM</td><td>13/11/2023</td><td>30</td><td>7:15 AM</td></tr>
<tr><td>13/11/2023</td><td>2</td><td>6:51 AM</td><td>13/11/2023</td><td>1</td><td>9:27 AM</td></tr>
<tr><td>14/11/2023</td><td>3</td><td>7:57 AM</td><td>14/11/2023</td><td>2</td><td>8:28 AM</td></tr>
<tr><td>15/11/2023</td><td>4</td><td>9:01 AM</td><td>15/11/2023</td><td>3</td><td>9:38 AM</td></tr>
<tr><td>16/11/2023</td><td>5</td><td>10:00 AM</td><td>16/11/2023</td><td>4</td><td>10:40 AM</td></tr>
<tr><td>17/11/2023</td><td>6</td><td>10:53 AM</td><td>17/11/2023</td><td>5</td><td>11:31 AM</td></tr>
<tr><td>18/11/2023</td><td>7</td><td>11:39 AM</td><td>18/11/2023</td><td>6</td><td>12:12 PM</td></tr>
<tr><td>19/11/2023</td><td>8</td><td>12:18 PM</td><td>19/11/2023</td><td>7</td><td>12:44 PM</td></tr>
<tr><td>20/11/2023</td><td>9</td><td>12:52 PM</td><td>20/11/2023</td><td>8</td><td>1:10 PM</td></tr>
<tr><td>21/11/2023</td><td>10</td><td>1:23 PM</td><td>21/11/2023</td><td>9</td><td>1:32 PM</td></tr>
<tr><td>22/11/2023</td><td>11</td><td>1:52 PM</td><td>22/11/2023</td><td>10</td><td>1:52 PM</td></tr>
<tr><td>23/11/2023</td><td>12</td><td>2:22 PM</td><td>23/11/2023</td><td>11</td><td>2:12 PM</td></tr>
<tr><td>24/11/2023</td><td>13</td><td>2:53 PM</td><td>24/11/2023</td><td>12</td><td>2:34 PM</td></tr>
<tr><td>25/11/2023</td><td>14</td><td>3:27 PM</td><td>25/11/2023</td><td>13</td><td>2:58 PM</td></tr>
<tr><td>26/11/2023</td><td>15</td><td>4:05 PM</td><td>26/11/2023</td><td>14</td><td>3:27 PM</td></tr>
<tr><td>27/11/2023</td><td>16</td><td>4:49 PM</td><td>27/11/2023</td><td>15</td><td>4:03 PM</td></tr>
<tr><td>28/11/2023</td><td>17</td><td>5:39 PM</td><td>28/11/2023</td><td>16</td><td>4:48 PM</td></tr>
<tr><td>29/11/2023</td><td>18</td><td>6:35 PM</td><td>29/11/2023</td><td>17</td><td>5:42 PM</td></tr>
<tr><td>30/11/2023</td><td>19</td><td>7:33 PM</td><td>30/11/2023</td><td>18</td><td>6:43 PM</td></tr>
</table>

You can find the description of each lunar day in the chapter "A Guide to The Moon Cycle and Lunar Days"

This month will demand patience from you, as well as responsibility and organizational skills. Remember, if you're going to do something, do it right.

Work. You are still busy working on big ideas, plans, and projects. In theory, all is well, but in practice, you will face some difficulties here.

Business owners and managers will be discovering that major construction or large-scale projects are not just a physical undertaking, but also do not come cheap. Seeking additional funds and negotiations over this difficult issue will likely be the backdrop of all of November, though the stars predict that your efforts will pay off – you will find the funding to cover the budget.

Closer to the end of November, you will be speaking more frequently with colleagues in other cities or abroad, and you might take a trip. You will see two different trends at play here – your relationship with certain colleagues will be progressing nicely, while with others, you will still have several challenges to overcome. If these issues began in the recent past, you will be grappling with them for some time to come.

Employees will be busy with day-to-day problems all month long, so they would be wise to take a few days off and focus on yourself. The stars recommend that you avoid approaching management unless you absolutely must and try to solve your problems on your own.

Money. November will not be an easy time for your bank account. You will be spending nonstop all month long. That may be related to work, or possibly your personal life.

When things get critical, however, you will be able to rely on your business partner or support from a loved one.

In the most extreme cases, you will need to take out a loan.

Love and family. Your personal life is turbulent, as well. You might face conflicts over difficult household issues. That is especially the case for those planning a major change, such as large repairs, or moving to a new house or apartment. If that sounds like you, you can expect disagreements over money and opposing opinions on the family budget. This is not critical, however, and things will fall into place by the end of the month.

Many couples may deal with challenges that arise when you and your partner disagree on the future of your relationship. This, along with all of the other stress surrounding November's events may leave you squabbling all month long.

Health. Those who manage to evade the personal and professional challenges of November might feel the pain when it comes to their health. Take care of yourself and avoid any infections or anything dangerous. The likelihood of injury or accident is very high this month.

December

New York Time			London Time		
Calendar Day	Lunar Day	Lunar Day Start Time	Calendar Day	Lunar Day	Lunar Day Start Time
01/12/2023	20	8:33 PM	01/12/2023	19	7:49 PM
02/12/2023	21	9:34 PM	02/12/2023	20	8:57 PM
03/12/2023	22	10:33 PM	03/12/2023	21	10:04 PM
04/12/2023	23	11:31 PM	04/12/2023	22	11:11 PM
06/12/2023	24	12:29 AM	06/12/2023	23	12:17 AM
07/12/2023	25	1:28 AM	07/12/2023	24	1:24 AM
08/12/2023	26	2:28 AM	08/12/2023	25	2:32 AM
09/12/2023	27	3:30 AM	09/12/2023	26	3:42 AM
10/12/2023	28	4:34 AM	10/12/2023	27	4:54 AM
11/12/2023	29	5:40 AM	11/12/2023	28	6:08 AM
12/12/2023	30	6:46 AM	12/12/2023	29	7:21 AM
12/12/2023	1	6:32 PM	12/12/2023	1	11:32 PM
13/12/2023	2	7:49 AM	13/12/2023	2	8:28 AM
14/12/2023	3	8:46 AM	14/12/2023	3	9:25 AM
15/12/2023	4	9:36 AM	15/12/2023	4	10:11 AM
16/12/2023	5	10:18 AM	16/12/2023	5	10:47 AM
17/12/2023	6	10:55 AM	17/12/2023	6	11:15 AM
18/12/2023	7	11:27 AM	18/12/2023	7	11:38 AM
19/12/2023	8	11:56 AM	19/12/2023	8	11:59 AM
20/12/2023	9	12:25 PM	20/12/2023	9	12:19 PM
21/12/2023	10	12:55 PM	21/12/2023	10	12:39 PM
22/12/2023	11	1:27 PM	22/12/2023	11	1:02 PM
23/12/2023	12	2:02 PM	23/12/2023	12	1:28 PM
24/12/2023	13	2:43 PM	24/12/2023	13	2:00 PM
25/12/2023	14	3:30 PM	25/12/2023	14	2:41 PM
26/12/2023	15	4:23 PM	26/12/2023	15	3:30 PM
27/12/2023	16	5:20 PM	27/12/2023	16	4:28 PM
28/12/2023	17	6:20 PM	28/12/2023	17	5:33 PM
29/12/2023	18	7:21 PM	29/12/2023	18	6:40 PM
30/12/2023	19	8:21 PM	30/12/2023	19	7:48 PM
31/12/2023	20	9:20 PM	31/12/2023	20	8:56 PM

You can find the description of each lunar day in the chapter "A Guide to The Moon Cycle and Lunar Days"

The last month of the year will have no shortage of emotional intensity for you. And though you can expect an obstacle course, you are sure to come out on top!

Work. You are still focused on big ideas, plans, and projects. In theory, things are still going well for you, but in practice, you might see some challenges in making all of that come to life. Some problems might pop up involving your colleagues in other cities or abroad, who may say one thing and then do another, but still imply something totally different altogether. Any administrative tasks will turn out to be complicated and are likely to require a lot more resources than you had initially planned.

From December 13 to January 2, Mercury will be in retrograde. This is the planet responsible for connections, and that means that a lot of setbacks are to be expected. During this time, be careful with the details, as well as with any financial documents, since any oversights here may lead to serious trouble down the road. That is relevant for both business owners and employees.

Regardless of how things look here, your business is moving ahead, and close to the end of the year, there will be no doubts of that.

Money. Your financial outlook is stable in December. You will have regular income and can expect the largest sums to come in at the end of the month, and on December 4-6, 8, 14, 15, 18, 22, 23, and 31.

Your expenses are also normal and may be related to business or possibly your personal life.

You might be negotiating over bonuses, financial benefits, or sponsorship. This is highly likely during the second half of the month, and things should work out your way.

Love and family. Your personal life is looking more peaceful and gentler this month. You might expect some arguments over money. However, they will gradually work themselves out, as the situation becomes less acute and pressing. If this involves home improvements, you might see clashing views over how to reach your goals and differing tastes.

Couples should avoid jealousy and gossip in December. Try to avoid saying something unless you are completely sure. Things are better that way.

Any travel planned for December should be carefully planned, especially during the second half of the month.

Health. This month, you are feeling energetic and have no reason to fear falling ill. However, all month long, the stars urge you to be careful when driving or traveling.

Aries Description

Sign. Masculine, fire, cardinal.

Rulers. Mars and Pluto in retrograde.

Exaltation. Sun.

Temperament. Choleric, impulsive, aggressive.

Positive traits. Logical, self-confident, decisive, determined, vigorous, persistence, proactive, entrepreneurial, ambitious, optimistic, dynamic.

Negative traits. Irritable, excitable, impulsive, intolerant, stubborn, grumpy, reckless, a tendency to exaggerate and sensationalize, unchecked passion, aggressive, despotic, tyrannical.

Weaknesses in the body. Head, brain, central nervous system, face, eyes, ears, teeth, tongue, nose, mouth, upper jaw, chin.

Metal. Iron.

Minerals. For a talisman, red jasper. Generally: rubies, carnet, diamond, Indian carnelian.

Numbers. 5, 7, 9.

Day. Tuesday.

Color. Red.

Aries's Energy

Aries opens the Zodiac and is first in the circle of signs. This is reflected in life, as Aries always tries to be first with everything – and he manages to do it, too! Aries is a fire sign, which symbolizes the material embodiment of the spirit, power, and transformation. In the trigon of fire signs, it is the first manifestation of cosmic fire – a fire of life that erupted, giving way to obsession and the desire to unleash one's natural potential.

Aries is ruled by Mars, which gives its children incredible energy reserves and enviable creativity. This planet is named for the mythological hero associated with victory and incredible powers; in ancient times, he was depicted as an angel with a magic sword cutting through the darkness. The energy of both Mars and Fire makes Aries the most active and powerful sign of the zodiac, with the greatest chances of conquering the highest mountains.

Astrological portrait of Aries

Anyone born under this sign believes in self-affirmation: "I am." He takes initiative and is a sure leader and moves forward, and doesn't worry about the consequences (those who follow will do that for you), guided by ideas that inspire and encourage – this is Aries' highest cosmic task.

Aries is symbolized by a ram, an animal that is direct and courageous as it tackles the challenges thrown at it by Fate. Aries are no different. They conquer the world with strength, assertiveness, and aggression. They are courageous and fearless. They cut straight to the chase, pushing any obstacles out of the way. Aries are never discouraged, they are always moving ahead as they dive into work with a passion, making waves, learn from the school of hard knocks, and in the end, are victorious.

To an Aries, life is a battlefield, and he is ready for anything, has no fear of insults or humiliation, and will not stop in the face of failure or difficulties. Fearlessness often drives an Aries to risk, and for the right cause, an Aries might even risk his or her life. But once in a crisis,

Aries has strong intuition, and therefore can rule and cope without any outside assistance.

All of Aries' excess fire makes him or her active, always striving to be the first and the best in everything, with a thirst for fame and recognition. Aries lights up at the sight of a new business and begins to radiate joy and electrify those around him. He is capable of leading large crowds with almost magical influence; this is why he is always in a position of power – either physical or psychological.

Aries is self-absorbed and views the world around him as an extension of himself. The feelings and interests of others are of little interest, and he does not know how to tap into the secrets of the human soul. It is not worth blaming him for that. Aries is able to succeed precisely because of this individualism. However, Aries has something that the other signs do not have – he is honest, noble, and absolutely sincere in every way. Lies and deceit are unknown to an Aries, which softens some of his selfishness. Another valuable quality is Aries' ability to always come to the rescue in times of suffering and need. He is a strong shoulder to lean on during tough times. Once Aries has lent a hand in a difficult time, he will do it again and again, though he may feel hurt if his own worries and concerns go unnoticed.

For all of Aries' bravery, assertiveness, and aggression, he is a very sensitive and defenseless child underneath. It is easy to insult or offend him. However, he quickly gets over any such attacks, as long as you provide him with praise and affection. Despite having a short fuse (Aries can descend into boorishness, scandal, and even fights), Aries will quickly walk away, and he will not waste much sulking before forgiving the offender, especially if he or she has a kind word to say about him.

But don't hold your breath waiting for an Aries to discover tact and the ability to smooth over disagreements and avoid outbursts. These qualities are not on his list of virtues. To an Aries, diplomacy means directness, ingenuity, and honesty. Thanks to their incredible work ethic, Aries tend to be wealthy, though they are never stingy and are willing to share it with others. After all, despite their selfishness, one of Aries' most fundamental needs is to bring joy to others. What's the point of wealth if there's no one to share it with?

How to recognize an Aries by appearances

There are two types of Aries: strong and muscular, or weak and sickly, which is what happens to them if they do not live in harmony with their sign, which requires a healthy diet and constant physical activity. Aries is lively in appearance, speaking quickly and in imperative tones, moving around decisively.

Aries is distinguished by a ruddy complexion. Mars, the red planet, bestows this on its children. Aries' face has a certain roughness, stiffness, and a pronounced nose. Aries women are somewhat masculine in their appearance, with a strong torso, broad shoulders, a narrow waist and hips, and a low, often hoarse voice.

Charting Aries' Fate

Generally speaking, Aries' fate is positive, though his path in life is unlikely to be called "smooth". There will be many changes, crises, and acute situations. Usually, Aries have had a restless youth and later settle down as adults. They always achieve anything they set their mind to, and their dreams and plans come true. But their success is theirs alone – Aries are workaholics, unafraid to take a risk, take great chances in life, and never fixate on past failures. They take Fate by the horns, and will not surrender, no matter what is thrown their way. They simply know no fear and ignore their failures. This, along with their self-confidence are Aries' trump cards.

Aries' impulsivity and scatterbrained nature may become obstacles to success. Aries is inspired by many ideas and perpetually rushing around and has a difficult time focusing on just one thing. They want to do it all, and right now. Therefore, they often do not see things through. The root cause of this is a lack of inner grounding and discipline; Aries is stubborn though and will replace them with stubbornness. He simply keeps charging forward, sometimes without even looking where he is going, until he is running into serious obstacles. In order to overcome this problem, he must:

• Find the right way to channel this energy into something inspiring.

• Create a set of behavioral rules for himself. He needs to be educated, have high standards for himself, but not be too strict, as being too hard one himself will be counterproductive), that is, to show both love and high standards at once, while occasionally indulging himself;

• learn to think first and have a clear behavioral standard. He can start small – count to 10 before saying or doing anything;

• Do away with black and white thinking – mine-yours, friend-enemy, good-bad) and expand his mind;

• Occasionally look within and reflect on his spiritual impulses and do a "debriefing". Aries is the only sign that does not fall into depression triggered by self-discovery.

A Guide to The Moon Cycle and Lunar Days

Since Ancient times, people have noticed that the moon has a strong influence on nature. Our Earth and everything living on it is a single living being, which is why the phases of the moon have such an effect on our health and mental state, and therefore, our lives. Remember Shakespeare and his description of Othello's jealousy in his famous tragedy:

"It is the very error of the moon, She comes more nearer Earth than she was wont And makes men mad."

If our inner rhythm is in harmony with that of the cosmos, we are able to achieve much more. People were aware of this a thousand years ago. The lunar calendar is ancient. We can find it among the ancient Sumerians (4000-3000 BC), the inhabitants of Mesopotamia, Native Americans, Hindus, and ancient Slavs. There is evidence that the Siberian Yakuts had a lunar calendar, as did the Malaysians.

Primitive tribes saw the moon as a source of fertility. Long before Christianity, the waxing moon was seen as favorable for planting new crops and starting a new business, for success and making money, while the waning moon was a sign that business would end.

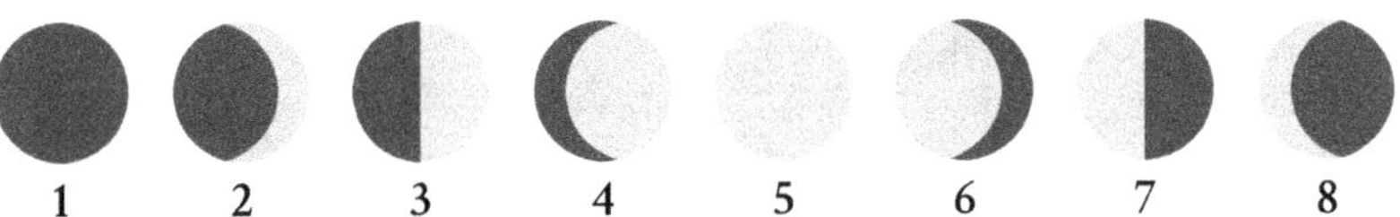

What are The Phases of The Moon?

- Phase 1 – new moon
- Phase 2 – waxing crescent moon
- Phase 3 – first quarter moon
- Phase 4 – waxing gibbous moon
- Phase 5 – full moon
- Phase 6 – waning gibbous moon
- Phase 7 – third quarter moon
- Phase 8 – waning crescent moon

To simplify things, we can divide the month into two phases:
Waxing crescent moon – before the full moon
Waning crescent moon – after the full moon

New Moon

We cannot see the new moon, as it is hidden. People might complain about feeling weak, mental imbalance, and fatigue. During this time, we want to avoid taking on too much or overdoing things. Generally, people are not very responsive and react poorly to requests, which is why it is best to look out for yourself, while not keeping your plate too full.

The new moon is a bad time for advertising – it will go unnoticed. It is not worth preparing any presentations, parties, or loud gatherings. People are feeling constrained, not very social, and sluggish.

This is also a less than ideal time for surgery, as your recovery will be slow, and the likelihood of medical error is high.

It is also difficult to get an accurate diagnosis during the new moon – diseases might seem to be hidden, and doctors might not see the real underlying cause of what ails you.

The new moon is also a bad time for dates, and sexual encounters may be dissatisfying and leave you feeling disappointed. Ancient astrologers did not advise planning a wedding night during the new moon.

Waxing Crescent Moon

It is easy to identify a waxing crescent moon. If you draw an imaginary line between the two "horns", you should see the letter P. The waxing moon is then divided into one and two quarters.

During the first quarter moon, we need to focus on planning – setting goals and thinking of how we will set about achieving them. However, it is still a good idea to hold back a bit and not overdo things. Energy levels are still low, though they are growing along with the moon. It is still a good idea to avoid any medical procedures during this time.

The second quarter is a time for bold, decisive action. Things will come easy, and there is a greater chance of a lucky break. This is a good time for weddings, especially if the moon will be in Libra, Cancer, or Taurus. Nevertheless, it is a good idea to put off any advertising activities and public speaking until closer to the full moon, if you can.

Full Moon

During the full moon, the Earth is located between the sun and the moon. During this time, the moon is round and fully illuminated. This takes place during days 14-16 of the lunar cycle.

During the full moon, many people feel more vigorous than usual. They are emotional, sociable, and actively seeking more contact, so this may be a good time for any celebrations.

However, be careful not to drink too much – you can relax to the point that you lose control, and the consequences of that can be very unpleasant. If you are able to stick to moderation, there is no better time for a party!

The full moon is also the best time for advertising, as not only will your campaign be widely seen, people will bc apt to remember it.

The full moon is also a favorable time for dates, and during this time, people are at their most open, romantic, and willing to tell each other something important that might take their relationship to the next level of trust and understanding.

Moreover, during the full moon, people feel a surge of energy, which may lead to hyperactivity, restlessness, and insomnia.

It will be harder to keep your emotions in check. You might face conflicts with friends, disasters, and accidents. During the full moon, any surgeries are **not a good idea**, as the risk of complications and bleeding is on the rise. Plastic surgery is also a bad idea, as swelling and bruises might be much worse than in another lunar phase. At the same time, the full moon is a good time to get an accurate diagnosis.

During this time, try to limit your calories and liquid intake (especially if you deal with bloating and excess weight), as your body is absorbing both calories and liquids faster during the full moon, and it can be very difficult to get rid of the weight later on.

Waning Crescent Moon

The full moon is over, and a new phase is beginning – the waning moon. This is a quieter time, when all of the jobs you started earlier are being partly or entirely completed (it all depends on the speed and scale).

Surgery will turn out much better if it is performed during the waning moon. Your recovery will be faster, and the likelihood of complications is much lower. If you have any plans to lose weight, the waning moon is the best time to do that. This is also a good time for quitting bad habits, such as smoking or cursing.

The waning moon can also be divided into the third and fourth quarters.

Third quarter - this is a favorable period, and you are able to resolve a lot of problems without conflict. People are calming down and ready to listen and take in information, while still being active. However, this is not the best time to begin any major projects, especially if you are unsure if you will be able to complete them by the start of the new lunar month.

The third quarter is a good time to get married, especially if the moon is in Cancer, Taurus, or Libra.

Fourth quarter – This is the most passive period of the lunar cycle. You are not as strong as usual. Your energy is lagging. You will be tired until reaching a new beginning. The best thing you can do as the lunar cycle comes to an end is to get things in order, and avoid anything that might get in your way at work or in personal relationships. Examine your successes and failures.

Now, let's discuss the lunar days in greater detail. For centuries, people around the world have described the influence of lunar days, and modern astrologers only add to this work, as they compare old texts to modern life.

The 1ˢᵗ lunar day

The first lunar day is extremely important for the rest of the lunar month. This is a much-needed day to carefully plan your activities and lay the groundwork for the rest of the lunar month. Remember that the first lunar day is not a good day for major activities, but rather for sitting down and planning things.

Avoid conflicts on this day, unless you want them to overshadow the rest of the month. Try to see the positive side of things and imagine that the lunar month will bring you good things both at work and in love. The more vividly you can imagine this, the sooner your desires will come to fruition. Perhaps it would be a good idea to jot down plans that will bring you closer to achieving your dreams. This is the best time for both manifesting and making wishes!

This is also a favorable day when it comes to seeking a new job or starting an academic program.

It is fine to go out on a date on the first lunar day, but limit any sexual contact, as your energy levels are low, and you are likely to end up disappointed.

Getting married on the first lunar day is not recommended.

Avoid getting a haircut – there are many indications that cutting your hair on the first lunar day will have a negative effect on your health and life expectancy.

Under no circumstances should you undergo any major cosmetic procedures, including plastic surgery. Energy levels are low, your skin is dull and almost stagnant. The results will not live up to your expectations, and in the worst-case scenario, you will end up looking worse than before. It is common for cosmetic procedures performed on this day to be disappointing or even useless. Even the best surgeons are less capable.

Your good dreams on the first lunar day foretell happiness and joy. Bad ones usually do not come true.

The 2nd lunar day

This is considered a lucky day, and is symbolized by a cornucopia. It is not an exaggeration to say that the second lunar day is a favorable time for both work and love. It is a time for action, and a great period to work on yourself, look for a new job, start something new, or complete any financial transaction, whether a sale or purchase. This is also a great time for creative and scientific insights, and a good time for any meeting – whether political or romantic.

Any romantic dates or sexual encounters during the second lunar day are unlikely to disappoint. This is also a good day for weddings or taking a trip with someone special.

During the second lunar day, the moon is beginning its waxing phase, which is a good time for anything you might to do nourish and restore your skin. This is a great time for any cosmetic procedures aimed at preservation, though it is best to put off any plastic surgery until the waning moon. If that is not possible, then the second lunar day is acceptable, if not ideal, and you will not run into any complications.

Folklore tells us that this is not a good day for a haircut, as that may lead to arguments with a loved one.

This is the best time for exercise – your body is in good shape, and you are able to handle new exercise regimens. If the moon happens to be in Scorpio, though, be careful.

This is a good day for anything positive, but avoid any conflicts, discussions about the status of your relationship, or litigation.

Dreams of the second lunar day are usually not prophetic.

Third 3rd day

On this day, we are usually able to make out a thin sliver of the lunar crescent. It is a longstanding tradition to show money during the new month – it is believed that as the moon grows, so will your savings.

However, astrological systems around the world consider this an unlucky, unfavorable day. It is not a good idea to travel, begin any new business, or give into your bad mood.

You might run into many a lot of problems at work on this day, which will cause you a lot of anxiety. However, it is a good day to take a step back and identify and set about fixing any flaws and shortcomings. Remember that everything tends to look worse on this day than it actually is.

It is not the time to ask management for anything – you are likely to walk away disappointed, and end up unfairly reprimanded rather than receiving a promotion or raise. Instead, focus on areas of work that need to be smoothed over or studied further. It will be clear what problems you are facing, and you will easily be able to find a remedy.

Do not rush to criticize your loved ones – things may not be as they appear. "Measure twice and cut once" is your motto on this day.

This is not a good day to get married, as the couple is likely to have a turbulent, short-lived marriage.

You can schedule a cosmetic procedure for this day, but only if it is relatively minor. Plastic surgery should wait.

Do exercises as usual, without overdoing it or adding any new routines.

Dreams on this day do not mean anything.

The 4th lunar day

These are relatively neutral days, in that they are unlikely to bring anything bad, but they also will not bring you any windfalls. The fourth lunar day is symbolized by a tree of paradise, the tree of knowledge, and the choice between good and evil. Things ultimately depend on us and our final decisions.

This is a great day for anything money-related – signing contracts, agreements, or even taking on credit. There are also a lot of contradictions on this day – on one hand, we are likely to receive money, which is a good thing, but on the other, we will have to give some of it away, which is never particularly fun or pleasant. There is good reason to consider all of your opportunities and possibilities before acting.

It is not a good day to get married, as the wedding will not be as fun as you had hoped. However, the fourth lunar day is, in fact, a good day for sex and conceiving a healthy child.

Be careful on this day if you happen to engage in any physical exercise, as it is not a good idea to overeat or abuse alcohol. Take care of yourself. Any illnesses which began on this day may be extremely dangerous, if they are not dealt with immediately.

Cosmetic procedures are not contraindicated, as long as they are to preserve your appearance. Plastic surgery can be performed if you truly feel it is necessary.

However, avoid getting a haircut, as it is unlikely to grow back healthily, and will become brittle and dull. However, if the moon is in Leo, you can disregard this advice.

Dreams may turn out to be real.

The 5th lunar day

Traditionally, the fifth lunar day is one of the worst of the lunar month. It is symbolized by a unicorn. Unicorns need to be tamed, but only a virgin is capable of doing so. Many people will feel drained on this day, or frustrated with themselves, those around them, and life in general.

Try to avoid arguments- any conflicts are likely to drag out for a long time, and then you may be overcome with guilt. This advice is relevant for both work and love.

Sexual encounters may be pleasant, but this is not a good day to plan a wedding, as it is likely to lead to a marriage full of unpleasant incidents.

Do not start any new businesses, or ask those around you for favors- you may be misunderstood and rejected.

It is fine to engage in physical exercise, but if you overdo it on this day, you may injure yourself.

Your energy levels are low. Cosmetic procedures may not be effective, and avoid any plastic surgeries.

It is good if you dream something connected with the road, trips or with movement in general. A bad dream might be a sign of a health problem which should be addressed.

The 6th lunar day

The symbol of the sixth lunar day is a cloud and a crane. This is a philosophical combination that suggests that it is not worth rushing things on these days. This is a very positive, lucky day for both work and love. Creative work will be especially successful, as will any attempts at opening a new business in your field.

The sixth lunar day is a good time for resolving any financial matters. There is one limitation, however – do not give anyone a loan, as they may not pay it back. But you can certainly sponsor and support those who are more vulnerable than you.

This day is a good time to go on a trip, whether close to home or far away.

This is also a good day for dates, weddings, and marriage proposals. Remember that energy is more romantic than sexual, so it is better to give the gift of roses and a bottle of champagne than hot, passionate sex.

It is a good idea to get some exercise, but do not overdo things, though you will probably not want to, either.

Cosmetic procedures will be successful, and you can even have plastic surgery performed, so long as the moon is not in Scorpio.

It is still a good idea to avoid getting your hair cut, as you might "cut off" something good in addition to your hair.

It is better to not discuss dreams as they are usually true. Your dreams of this day can remind you of something that needs to be completed as soon as possible.

The 7ᵗʰ lunar day

This is also a favorable lunar day, and it is symbolized by a fighting cock, which is an Avestan deity. Avoid any aggression on this day, and instead work on yourself, spend time at home or in nature. Avoid discussing the status of your relationship with anyone, arguing, or wishing bad things on anyone. Everything will come back to haunt you, remember, silence is golden.

Business negotiations and contracts will be successful. You can find support, sponsors, and people ready to help you in both words and deeds.

Lighten up with your colleagues and subordinates. Pay attention not only to their shortcomings, but also to their skills. This is a good day for reconciliation and creating both political and romantic unions.

The seventh lunar day is good for traveling, no matter how near or far from home.

It is also a favorable time for love and marriage.

Exercise moderately, and any plastic surgeries will go very smoothly, as long as the moon is not in Scorpio.

Dreams of this day may become a reality.

The 8ᵗʰ lunar day

The symbol for this day is a Phoenix, which symbolizes eternal rebirth and renewal, because this day is a great time for changes in all areas of your life. Your energy is likely to be high, and you want to do something new and unusual. This is a good time to look for a new job or begin studying something. Any out-of-the-box thinking is welcome, along with shaking things up a bit in order to improve your life.

However, avoid any financial transactions, as you may incur losses.

Avoid aggression. You can share your opinion by presenting well-founded arguments and facts, instead.

The phoenix rises from the ashes, so this is a good time to be careful with electrical appliances and fire in general. The risk of housefires is high.

Avoid any major financial transactions on the eighth day, as you may end up facing a series of complications. You can pay people their salaries, as this is unlikely to be a large sum.

This is a good day for weddings, but only if you and your future spouse are restless, creative souls and hope to achieve personal development through your marriage.

Any cosmetic procedures and plastic surgeries will go well today, as they are related to rebirth and renewal. Surgeons may find that they are true artists on this day!

You can try to change your hairstyle and get a fashionable haircut on this day.

You can trust your dreams seen on this day.

The 9th lunar day

The ninth lunar day is not particularly auspicious, and is even referred to as "Satan's" day. You may be overcome with doubt, suspicions, even depression and conflicts.

Your self-esteem will suffer, so don't overdo things physically, and avoid overeating or abusing alcohol.

This is a negative day for any business deals, travel, or financial transactions.

This is a particularly bad day for any events, so keep your head down at work and avoid any new initiatives.

It is better to avoid getting married on "Satan's" day, as the marriage will not last very long. Avoid sex, as well, but you can take care of your partner, listen them, and support them however they need.

Any cosmetic procedures will not have a lasting effect, and avoid any plastic surgery. A haircut will not turn out as you hoped.

Dreams of this day are usually prophetic.

The 10th lunar day

This is one of the luckiest days of the lunar month. It is symbolized by a spring, mushroom, or phallus. This is a time for starting a new business, learning new things, and creating.

The 10th lunar day is particularly lucky for business. Networking and financial transactions will be a success and bring hope. This is an ideal time for changing jobs, shifting your business tactics, and other renewals.

This is a perfect time for people in creative fields and those working in science, who may come up with incredible ideas that will bring many successful returns.

This is a very successful day for building a family and proposing marriage. This is a good time for celebrations and communication, so plan parties, meet with friends, and plan a romantic date.

One of the symbols for this day is a phallus, so sexual encounters are likely to be particularly satisfying.

The 10th lunar day is the best time to begin repairs, buying furniture, and items for home improvement.

You can exercise vigorously, and cosmetic procedures and plastic surgery will be very effective.

Dreams of this day will not come true.

The 11ᵗʰ lunar day

This is one of the best lunar days, and seen as the pinnacle of the lunar cycle. People are likely to be energetic, enthusiastic, and ready to move forward toward their goals.

The 11ᵗʰ lunar day is very successful for any financial transactions or business deals and meetings.

You might actively make yourself known, approach management to discuss a promotion, or look for a new job. This is an auspicious time for advertising campaigns, performances, and holding meetings.

Any trips planned will be a great success, whether near or far from home.

Romantic relationships are improving, sex is harmonious, and very desired.

Weddings held on this day will be fun, and the marriage will be a source of joy and happiness.

Exercise is a great idea, and you might even beat your own personal record.

This is an ideal time for any cosmetic procedures, but any more serious plastic surgeries might lead to a lot of bruising and swelling.

A haircut will turn out as you had hoped, and you can experiment a bit with your appearance.

You can ignore dreams of this day – usually they do not mean anything.

The 12th lunar day

This day is symbolized by the Grail and a heart. As we move closer to the full moon, our emotions are at their most open. During this time, if you ask someone for something, your request will be heeded. This is a day of faith, goodness, and divine revelations.

For business and financial transactions, this is not the most promising day. However, if you help others on this day, your good deeds are sure to come back to you.

This is a day for reconciliation, so do not try to explain your relationships, as no one is at fault, and it is better to focus on yourself, anyway.

Avoid weddings and sex on this day, but if you want to do what your partner asks, there is no better time.

Many may feel less than confident and cheerful during this day, so take it easy when working out. Avoid overeating, stay hydrated, and avoid alcohol.

The 12th lunar day is not the best for getting married or having sex, but the stars would welcome affection and a kind word.

Avoid getting a haircut, or any plastic surgeries. This is a neutral day for minor cosmetic procedures.

Nearly all dreams will come true.

The 13th lunar day

This day is symbolized by Samsara, the wheel of fate, which is very erratic and capable of moving in any direction. This is why the 13th lunar day is full of contradictions. In Indian traditions, this day is compared to a snake eating its own tail. This is a day for paying off old debts and returning to unfinished business.

Avoid beginning any new business on this day. It is preferable to finish old tasks and proofread your work. Information you receive on this day may not be reliable and must be verified.

It is worth resolving financial problems very carefully, and avoid arguments and conflict.

Do not change jobs on this day or go to a new place for the first time. Do not sit at home alone, though, go see old friends, parents, or older family members.

Minor cosmetic procedures are welcome on this day, but avoid any plastic surgery, as you may experience major swelling and bruising. Avoid any haircuts, too.

As a rule, all dreams will come true.

The 14th lunar day

It's a full moon! The 14th lunar day is one of the happiest, and it is symbolized by the trumpet. Pay attention – you may run into new, much-needed information. Networking will be successful, and you can confidently sign agreements, meet with people, and attend fun gatherings or other leisure activities. This is one of the best days for advertising, performances, and concerts, and those working in creative professions should keep this in mind, as should those who work in politics. Do not sit in place on this day – you need to get out and see others, make new connections, and try to be visible.

This is one of the best days for communication with and making requests from management, as your initiatives will be noticed and welcome. You might talk about a promotion, raise, or something similarly related to professional growth.

Couples will see their relationship is moving along well on this day, and it is also a good day for getting married.

Any sex on this day will be vigorous and memorable for a long time. The full moon is the best time for conceiving a child.

Any cosmetic procedures will be effective, but avoid any major changes to your appearance, as there is a high likelihood of bleeding and bruising. A haircut will turn out well.

Your dreams of this day will be more or less doubtful.

The 15th lunar day

It's a full moon! This day is symbolized by a serpent of fire. This is the energy peak of the entire lunar cycle, and a lot will depend on where you are focusing your energy.

You might face a lot of temptations on this day, for example, you might tell someone else's secret or your own to others, and come to regret it for a long time. The stars suggest exercising restraint in both your words and actions, as the 15th day of the lunar cycle is a day of deception and weaknesses.

This is a very active time, and many people might take unnecessary risks. This is not the best day for signing any agreements or contracts. For any performances, concerts, or advertising, however, this is one of the best days of the month.

You can get married on the 15th day, but only if you know each other well and have carefully considered your partnership, without any hasty decisions. This is also a favorable day for a second marriage.

Your romantic relationship is looking wonderful – you are on cloud 9, writing poetry, and deeply convinced of how right your partner is for you – and they feel the same way. It is important that this does not suddenly lead to an abrupt disappointment.

Avoid getting any haircuts on the 15th day of the month, as you may end up with a headache.

Conservative cosmetic procedures and creams will be very effective, but avoid any injections or plastic surgery today. Bleeding, swelling, and bruising are all but guaranteed.

Dreams on the 15th day nearly always come true.

The 16th lunar day

This day is symbolized by a dove. The full moon is over, and the moon is now in its waning phase. Usually, after the turbulent days of the full moon, people feel a bit under the weather. They are not cheerful, and want to avoid excess worry and give themselves a chance to breathe.

Don't ignore your body's wishes, take it easy with physical activities, and take some time for yourself. You might spend time in nature, in the forest, or at a country home.

The 16th day of the lunar month is a time for moderation in all areas – your behavior, eating, and even in your clothes. If you overate during the full moon period, now is the time to diet a bit or at least avoid fatty foods and meat.

This is not a promising day for resolving any financial matters. Keep your documents in order and get ready for any future meetings, instead. If you help a loved one, your good deed will come back 100 times over.

Avoid getting married today, as well as sex.

Cosmetic procedures are likely to be a success, especially if they are related to cleansing your skin, but it is best to avoid any plastic surgery or injections. Your body is not ready to accept them. A haircut will turn out as you hoped.

Any dreams are likely to come true, but that also depends on a correct interpretation.

The 17th lunar day

This day is represented by a vine and bell. It is a happy day and both successful and fun-filled. It is also a good time for negotiations, concluding small business deals, shaking up staffing, and creativity. However, you should keep in mind that the 17th day is only favorable for minor business, and you should avoid starting any major events.

Avoid any major financial transactions on this day. Do not give anyone money as a loan or borrow anything yourself, either.

Any travel, whether for business or pleasure, is likely to be a success.

The 17th day is a great time to get married, and an ideal day for dates. Any sexual encounters will bring you happiness and joy.

Avoid getting your hair cut on this day, but cosmetic procedures and plastic surgery will be a success. Women will look better than usual.

Your dreams are likely to come true in three days.

The 18th lunar day

This day is represented by a mirror. It is a difficult, and generally unpromising day, too. Just as the mirror reflects our imperfections back to us, we need to remember that moderation and modesty are key.

The 18th day is not a favorable time for any business meetings or financial transactions. You can, however work on jobs you already began. It is, however, a positive day for those who work in research or the creative fields.

Your motto of the day is to keep a cool head when it comes to your opportunities and the opportunities of those around you. This is relevant for both work and romantic relationships. It is not a good time to criticize others – any conflicts or arguments may lead to lasting consequences, which you do not need.

Avoid getting married on this day, as well as sexual encounters, which are likely to be disappointing. It is a good time to take a trip together, which will only be good for your relationship.

Avoid getting your hair cut, though this is a relatively neutral day for a haircut, which might turn out well, and though it will not exceed your expectations, it will also not leave you upset. Avoid any plastic surgeries.

Dreams on this day will come true.

The 19th lunar day

This is a very difficult day and it is represented by a spider. The energy is complicated, if not outright dangerous. Don't panic or get depressed, though – this is a test of your strength, and if you are able to hold onto all you have achieved. This is relevant for both work and love. On the 19th day, you should avoid taking any trips.

The energy of the 19th lunar day is very unfavorable for beginning any major projects, and business in general. Work on what you started earlier, get your affairs in order, think over your ideas and emotions, and check to make sure that everything you have done hitherto is living up to your expectations. Do not carry out any financial transactions or take out any loans – do not loan anyone else money, either. Do not ask your managers for anything as they are unlikely to listen to what you have to say, and make judgments instead.

This is a day when you might face outright deception, so do not take any risks and ignore rumors. Do not work on anything related to real estate or legal matters.

This is a very hard time for people with an unbalanced psyche, as they may experience sudden exacerbations or even suicidal ideations.

This is a very unlucky day to get married. Sexual encounters might be disappointing and significantly worsen your relationship.

Avoid any haircuts or cosmetic procedures or surgeries.

Your dreams of this day will come true.

The 20th lunar day

This is also a difficult day, though less so than the 19th. It is represented by an eagle. This is a good time to work on your own development and spiritual growth, by speaking to a psychologist or astrologer.

Avoid pride, anger, arrogance, and envy.

The 20th lunar day is a good time for people who are active and decisive. They will be able to easily overcome any obstacles, flying over them just like an eagle. If you have to overcome your own fears, you will be able to do so – don't limit yourself, and you will see that there is nothing to be afraid of. It is a good day for any financial transactions, signing contracts, and reaching agreements, as well as networking.

The 20th lunar day is a favorable time for those who work in the creative fields, as they will be able to dream up the idea that will open up a whole host of new possibilities. Avoid conflicts – they may ruin your relationship with a lot of people, and it will not be easy to come back from that.

This is a lucky day for getting married, but only if you have been with your partner for several years, now. Sexual encounters will not be particularly joyful, but they also will not cause you any problems.

Avoid getting your hair cut, but you can certainly get it styled. The 20th lunar day is a good day for those who are looking to lose weight. You will be able to do so quickly, and it will be easy for you to follow a diet.

Cosmetic procedures will be a success, as will any plastic surgeries.

Pay attention to dreams of this day as they are likely to come true.

The 21st lunar day

This is one of the most successful days of the lunar month, and it is symbolized by a herd of horses – imagine energy, strength, speed, and bravery. Everything you think up will happen quickly, and you will be able to easily overcome obstacles. A mare is not only brave but also an honest animal, so you will only experience this luck if you remember that honesty is always the best policy.

This is also a favorable day for business. Reaching new agreements and signing contracts, or dealing with foreign partners – it is all likely to be a success. Any financial issues will be resolved successfully.

Those in the creative world will be able to show off their talent and be recognized for their work. Anyone involved in the performing arts can expect success, luck, and recognition. A galloping herd of horses moves quickly, so you might transition to a new job, move to a new apartment, or go on a business trip or travel with your better half.

The 21st lunar day is one of the best to get married or have a sexual encounter.

This is a great time for athletes, hunters, and anyone who likes adventurous activities.

But for criminals and thieves, this is not a lucky or happy day – they will quickly be brought to justice.

Any haircuts or cosmetic procedures are likely to be a huge success and bring both beauty and happiness. You will recover quickly after any surgeries, perhaps without any swelling or bruising at all.

Dreams tend to not be reliable.

The 22nd lunar day

This day will be strange and contradictory. It is symbolized by the elephant Ganesha. According to Indian mythology, Ganesha is the patron saint of hidden knowledge. so this is a favorable day for anyone who is trying to learn more about the world and ready to find the truth, though this is often seen as a hopeless endeavor. This is a day for philosophers and wisemen and women. However, it is an inauspicious day for business, and unlikely to lead to resolving financial issues, signing contracts, agreements, or beginning new projects. You can expect trouble at work.

For creative people, and new employees, this is a successful day.

This is a good day for apologies and reconciliation.

Avoid getting married, though you can feel free to engage in sexual encounters.

For haircuts and cosmetic procedures, this is a fantastic day. Surgeries will also turn out, as long as the moon is not in Scorpio.

Dreams will come true.

The 23rd lunar day

This is a challenging day represented by a crocodile, which is a very aggressive animal. This is a day of strong energy, but it is also adventurous and tough. Your main task is to focus your energy in the right direction. There may be accidents, arguments, conflicts, fights, and violence, which is why it is important to strive for balance and calm.

Keep a close eye on your surroundings – there may be traitors or people who do not wish you well, so be careful.

However, this is still a favorable day for business – many problems will be resolved successfully. You are able to sign contracts and receive credit successfully, as long as you remain active and decisive in what you do.

This is not a day for changing jobs or working on real estate transactions or legal proceedings. This is not a favorable day for traveling, no matter how near or far you plan on going.

This is not a promising day to get married – things may end in conflict, if not an all-out brawl.

Sexual relations are not off the table, as long as the couple trusts one another.

Haircuts or cosmetic procedures will not turn out as you had hoped, so avoid them.

Dreams during this lunar day usually mean something opposite of what awaits you, so you can disregard them.

The 24th lunar day

This is a neutral, calm day that is symbolized by a bear. It is favorable for forgiveness and reconciliation.

This is also a good day for learning new things, reading, self-development, and taking time to relax in nature.

This is a great day for any type of financial activity, conferences, academic meetings, and faraway travel.

The 24th lunar day is a good time for love and getting married, as any marriage will be strong and lasting.

Cosmetic procedures and plastic surgery will be a success, and you can expect a speedy recovery.

Avoid getting a haircut on this day, however, as your hair will likely thin and grow back slowly.

Dreams of this lunar day are usually connected with your personal life.

The 25th lunar day

This is still another quiet day, symbolized by a turtle.

Just like a turtle, this is not a day to rush, and it is best to sit down and take stock of your life. This is a good time for resolving any personal problems, as the moon's energy makes it possible for you to calm down and find the right path.

This is also not a bad day for business. It is believed that any business you begin on this day is sure to be a success. This is especially the case for trade and any monetary activities.

The 25th lunar day is not a good day to get married, especially if the couple is very young.

This is a neutral day for sexual encounters, as the moon is waning, energy is low, so the decision is yours.

Avoid any cosmetic procedures, except those for cleansing your skin. This is not a favorable day for haircuts or plastic surgery – unless the moon is in Libra or Leo.

You can have a prophetic dream on this day.

The 26th lunar day

The 26th lunar day is full of contradictions and complicated. It is represented by a toad.

It is not time to start or take on something new, as nothing good will come of it. Avoid any major purchases, as you will later come to see that your money was wasted. The best thing you can do on this day is stay at home and watch a good movie or read a good book.

Avoid traveling on this day, as it may not turn out well.

The 26th lunar day is a negative day for any business negotiations and starting new businesses. Do not complete any business deals or financial transactions. Your colleagues may be arguing, and your managers may be dissatisfied. But if you have decided to leave your job, there is no better time to do so.

This is not a good day to get married, as both partners' expectations may fall flat, and they will soon be disappointed.

The waning moon carries a negative charge, so avoid any haircuts and surgeries, though you can get cosmetic procedures if they are relatively minor.

Your dreams will come true.

The 27th lunar day

The 27th lunar day is one of the best days of the month, and it is represented by a ship. You can boldly start any new business, which is sure to be promising. This is a great day for students, teachers, and learning new things. Any information that comes to you on this day may be extremely valuable and useful to you.

The 27th day is good for communication and travel, whether near or far from home, and no matter whether it is for work or pleasure.

This is also a good day for any professional activities or financial transactions. If there are people around you who need help, you must support them, as your good deeds will come back 100-fold.

Romantic dates will go well, though any weddings should be quiet and subdued. This is a particularly good day for older couples or second marriages.

The waning moon means that hair will grow back very slowly, but in general, you can expect a haircut to turn out well. This is a great day for plastic surgery or cosmetic procedures, as the results will be pleasing, and you will have a speedy recovery, without any bruising or swelling, most of the time.

However, beware if the moon is in Scorpio on this day – that is not a good omen for any plastic surgery.

Do not pay any attention to dreams on this day.

The 28th lunar day

This is another favorable day in the waning moon cycle, and it is represented by a lotus. This is a day of wisdom and spiritual awakening. If possible, spend part of the day in nature. It is important to take stock of the last month and decide what you need to do during its two remaining days.

This is a good time for any career development, changing jobs, conducting business, decision-making, and signing agreements, as well as going on a trip. You might conclude any business deal, hold negotiations, work with money and securities.

This is also a good day for any repairs or improvements around your home or apartment.

Anyweddingstodayshouldbesubduedandmodest,andrestrictedtofamily members only. A loud, raucous wedding might not turn out very well. Your hair will grow slowly, but any haircuts will turn out very elegant and stylish. Cosmetic procedures and surgeries are not contraindicated. You will recover quickly with little bruising and swelling.

Do not take any dreams too seriously.

The 29th lunar day

This is one of the most difficult days of the lunar month, and it is considered a Satanic day, unlucky for everyone and everything. It is symbolized by an octopus.

This is a dark day, and many will feel melancholy, depression, and a desire to simply be left alone. This is a day full of conflict and injuries, so be careful everywhere and with everyone. If you can, avoid any travel, and be particularly careful when handling any sharp objects. Do not engage in any business negotiations, sign any contracts, or take part in any networking.

Astrologers believe that anything you start on this day will completely fall apart. For once and for all, get rid of things that are impeding you from living your life. This is a good time to avoid people who you do find unpleasant.

This is also a time for fasting and limitations for everyone. Do not hold any celebrations, weddings, or have sexual relations – these events may not turn out as you hoped, and instead bring you nothing but suffering and strife.

Avoid getting a haircut, as well, as it will not make you look more beautiful and your hair will come back lifeless and dull. Cosmetic procedures can go ahead, but avoid any surgeries.

Dreams are likely to be true.

The 30th lunar day

There is not always a 30th lunar day, as some lunar months have only 29 days. This day is represented by a swan. The 30th lunar day is usually very short, and sometimes, it lasts less than an hour. This is a time for forgiveness and calm.

You might take stock of the last month, while also avoiding anything you do not need around you. Pay back loans, make donations, reconcile with those who recently offended you, and stop speaking to people who cause you suffering.

This is a good time for tying up loose ends, and many astrologers believe that it is also a good day to start new business.

However, avoid celebrations or weddings on this day. Spouses will either not live long, or they will quickly grow apart.

Do not get a haircut on this day, though cosmetic procedures are possible, as long as you avoid any surgeries.

Dreams promise happiness and should come true.

A Guide to Zodiac Compatibility

Often, when we meet a person, we get a feeling that they are good and we take an instant liking to them. Another person, however, gives us immediate feelings of distrust, fear and hostility. Is there an astrological reason why people say that 'the first impression is the most accurate'? How can we detect those who will bring us nothing but trouble and unhappiness?

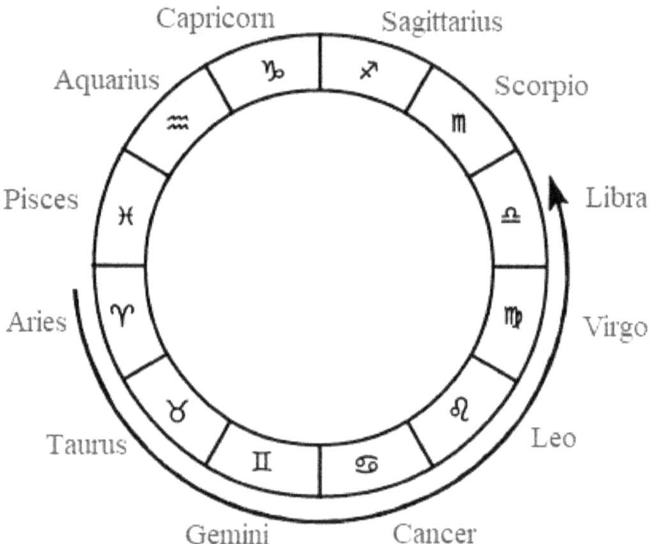

Without going too deeply into astrological subtleties unfamiliar to some readers, it is possible to determine the traits according to which friendship, love or business relationships will develop.

Let's begin with problematic relationships - our most difficult are with our **8th sign**. For example, for Aries the 8th sign is Scorpio, for Taurus it is Sagittarius and so on. Finding your 8th sign is easy; assume your own sign to be first (see above Figure) and then move eight signs counter clockwise around the Zodiac circle. This is also how the other signs (fourth, ninth and so on) that we mention are to be found.

Ancient astrologers variously referred to the 8th sign as the symbol of death, of destruction, of fated love or unfathomable attraction. In astrological terms, this pair is called 'master and slave' or 'boa constrictor and rabbit', with the role of 'master' or 'boa constrictor' being played by our 8th sign.

This relationship is especially difficult for politicians and business people.

We can take the example of a recent political confrontation in the USA. Hilary Clinton is a Scorpio while Donald Trump is a Gemini - her 8th sign. Even though many were certain that Clinton would be elected President, she lost.

To take another example, Hitler was a Taurus and his opponents – Stalin and Churchill - were both of his 8th sign, Sagittarius. The result of their confrontation is well known. Interestingly, the Russian Marshals who dealt crushing military blows to Hitler and so helped end the Third Reich - Konstantin Rokossovsky and Georgy Zhukov - were also Sagittarian, Hitler's 8th sign.

In another historical illustration, Lenin was also a Taurus. Stalin was of Lenin's 8th sign and was ultimately responsible for the downfall and possibly death of his one-time comrade-in-arms.

Business ties with those of our 8th sign are hazardous as they ultimately lead to stress and loss; both financial and moral. So, do not tangle with your 8th sign and never fight with it - your chances of winning are remote!

Such relationships are very interesting in terms of love and romance, however. We are magnetically attracted to our 8th sign and even though it may be very intense physically, it is very difficult for family life;

'Feeling bad when together, feeling worse when apart'.

As an example, let us take the famous lovers - George Sand who was Cancer and Alfred de Musset who was Sagittarius. Cancer is the 8th sign for Sagittarius, and the story of their crazy two-year love affair was the subject of much attention throughout France. Critics and writers were divided into 'Mussulist' and 'Sandist' camps; they debated fiercely about who was to blame for the sad ending to their love story - him or her. It's hard to imagine the energy needed to captivate the public for so long, but that energy was destructive for the couple. Passion raged in their hearts, but neither of them was able to comprehend their situation.

Georges Sand wrote to Musset, "*I don't love you anymore, and I will always adore you. I don't want you anymore, and I can't do without you. It seems that nothing but a heavenly lightning strike can heal me by destroying me. Good-bye! Stay or go, but don't say that I am not suffering. This is the only thing that can make me suffer even more, my love, my life, my blood! Go away, but kill me, leaving.*" Musset replied only in brief, but its power surpassed Sand's tirade, "*When you embraced me, I felt something that is still bothering me, making it impossible for me to approach another woman.*" These two people loved each other passionately and for two years lived together in a powder keg of passion, hatred and treachery.

When someone enters into a romantic liaison with their 8th sign, there will be no peace; indeed, these relationships are very attractive to those who enjoy the edgy, the borderline and, in the Dostoevsky style, the melodramatic. The first to lose interest in the relationship is, as a rule, the 8th sign.

If, by turn of fate, our child is born under our 8th sign, they will be very different from us and, in some ways, not live up to our expectations. It may be best to let them choose their own path.

In business and political relationships, the combination with our **12th sign** is also a complicated one.

We can take two political examples. Angela Merkel is a Cancer while Donald Trump is a Gemini - her 12th sign. This is why their relations are strained and complicated and we can even perhaps assume that the American president will achieve his political goals at her expense. Boris Yeltsin (Aquarius) was the 12th sign to Mikhail Gorbachev (Pisces) and it was Yeltsin who managed to dethrone the champion of Perestroika.

Even ancient astrologers noticed that our relationships with our 12th signs can never develop evenly; it is one of the most curious and problematic combinations. They are our hidden enemies and they seem to be digging a hole for us; they ingratiate themselves with us, discover our innermost secrets. As a result, we become bewildered and make mistakes when we deal with them. Among the Roman emperors murdered by members of their entourage, there was an interesting pattern - all the murderers were the 12th sign of the murdered.

We can also see this pernicious effect in Russian history: the German princess Alexandra (Gemini) married the last Russian Tsar Nicholas II (Taurus) - he was her 12th sign and brought her a tragic death. The wicked genius Grigory Rasputin (Cancer) made friends with Tsarina Alexandra, who was his 12th sign, and was murdered as a result of their odd friendship. The weakness of Nicholas II was exposed, and his authority reduced after the death of the economic and social reformer Pyotr Stolypin, who was his 12th sign. Thus, we see a chain of people whose downfall was brought about by their 12th sign.

So, it makes sense to be cautious of your 12th sign, especially if you have business ties. Usually, these people know much more about us than we want them to and they will often reveal our secrets for personal gain if it suits them. However, the outset of these relationships is, as a rule, quite normal - sometimes the two people will be friends, but sooner or later one will betray the other one or divulge a secret; inadvertently or not.

In terms of romantic relationships, our 12th sign is gentle, they take care of us and are tender towards us. They know our weaknesses well but accept them with understanding. It is they who guide us, although sometimes almost imperceptibly. Sexual attraction is usually strong.

For example, Meghan Markle is a Leo, the 12th sign for Prince Harry, who is a Virgo. Despite Queen Elizabeth II being lukewarm about the match, Harry's love was so strong that they did marry.

If a child is our 12th sign, it later becomes clear that they know all our secrets, even those that they are not supposed to know. It is very difficult to control them as they do everything in their own way.

Relations with our **7th sign** are also interesting. They are like our opposite; they have something to learn from us while we, in turn, have something to learn from them. This combination, in business and personal relationships, can be very positive and stimulating provided that both partners are quite intelligent and have high moral standards but if not, constant misunderstandings and challenges follow. Marriage or co-operation with the 7th sign can only exist as the union of two fully-fledged individuals and in this case love, significant business achievements and social success are possible.

However, the combination can be not only interesting, but also quite complicated.

An example is Angelina Jolie, a Gemini, and Brad Pitt, a Sagittarius. This is a typical bond with a 7th sign - it's lively and interesting, but rather stressful. Although such a couple may quarrel and even part from time to time, never do they lose interest in each other.

This may be why this combination is more stable in middle-age when there is an understanding of the true nature of marriage and partnership. In global, political terms, this suggests a state of eternal tension - a cold war - for example between Yeltsin (Aquarius) and Bill Clinton (Leo).

Relations with our **9th sign** are very good; they are our teacher and advisor - one who reveals things we are unaware of and our relationships with them very often involve travel or re-location. The combination can lead to spiritual growth and can be beneficial in terms of business.

Although, for example, Trump and Putin are political opponents, they can come to an understanding and even feel a certain sympathy for each other because Putin is a Libra while Trump is a Gemini, his 9th sign.

This union is also quite harmonious for conjugal and romantic relationships.

We treat our **3rd sign** somewhat condescendingly. They are like our younger siblings; we teach them and expect them to listen attentively. Our younger brothers and sisters are more often than not born under this sign. In terms of personal and sexual relationships, the union is not very inspiring and can end quickly, although this is not always the case. In terms of business, it is fairly average as it often connects partners from different cities or countries.

We treat our **5th sign** as a child and we must take care of them accordingly. The combination is not very good for business, however, since our 5th sign triumphs over us in terms of connections and finances, and thereby gives us very little in return save for love or sympathy. However, they are very good for family and romantic relationships, especially if the 5th sign is female. If a child is born as a 5th sign to their parents, their relationship will be a mutually smooth, loving and understanding one that lasts a lifetime.

Our **10th sign** is a born leader. Depending on the spiritual level of those involved, both pleasant and tense relations are possible; the relationship is often mutually beneficial in the good times but mutually disruptive in the bad times. In family relations, our 10th sign always tries to lead and will do so according to their intelligence and upbringing.

Our **4th sign** protects our home and can act as a sponsor to strengthen our financial or moral positions. Their advice should be heeded in all cases as it can be very effective, albeit very unobtrusive. If a woman takes this role, the relationship can be long and romantic, since all the spouse's wishes are usually met one way or another. Sometimes, such couples achieve great social success; for instance, Hilary Clinton, a Scorpio is the 4th sign to Bill Clinton, a Leo. On the other hand, if the husband is the 4th sign for his wife, he tends to be henpecked. There is often a strong sexual attraction. Our 4th sign can improve our living conditions and care for us in a parental way. If a child is our 4th sign, they are close to us and support us affectionately.

Relations with our **11th sign** are often either friendly or patronizing; we treat them reverently, while they treat us with friendly condescension. Sometimes, these relationships develop in an 'older brother' or 'high-ranking friend' sense; indeed, older brothers and sisters are often our 11th sign. In terms of personal and sexual relationships, our 11th sign is always inclined to enslave us. This tendency is most clearly manifested in such alliances as Capricorn and Pisces or Leo and Libra. A child who is the 11th sign to their parents will achieve greater success than their parents, but this will only make the parents proud.

Our **2nd sign** should bring us financial or other benefits; we receive a lot from them in both our business and our family life. In married couples, the 2nd sign usually looks after the financial situation for the benefit of the family. Sexual attraction is strong.

Our **6th sign** is our 'slave'; we always benefit from working with them and it's very difficult for them to escape our influence. In the event of hostility, especially if they have provoked the conflict, they receive a powerful retaliatory strike. In personal relations, we can almost destroy them by making them dance to our tune. For example, if a husband doesn't allow his wife to work or there are other adverse family circumstances, she gradually becomes lost as an individual despite being surrounded by care. This is the best-case scenario; worse outcomes are possible. Our 6th sign has a strong sexual attraction to us because we are the fatal 8th sign for them; we cool down quickly, however, and often make all kinds of demands. If the relationship with our 6th sign is a long one, there is a danger that routine, boredom and stagnation will ultimately destroy the relationship. A child born under our 6th sign needs particularly careful handling as they can feel fear or embarrassment when communicating with us. Their health often needs increased attention and we should also remember that they are very different from us emotionally.

Finally, we turn to relations with **our own sign**. Scorpio with Scorpio and Cancer with Cancer get along well, but in most other cases, however, our own sign is of little interest to us as it has a similar energy. Sometimes, this relationship can develop as a rivalry, either in business or in love.

There is another interesting detail - we are often attracted to one particular sign. For example, a man's wife and mistress often have the same sign. If there is confrontation between the two, the stronger character displaces the weaker one. As an example, Prince Charles is a Scorpio, while both Princess Diana and Camilla Parker Bowles were born under the sign of Cancer. Camilla was the more assertive and became dominant.

Of course, in order to draw any definitive conclusions, we need an individually prepared horoscope, but the above always, one way or another, manifests itself.

Love Description of Zodiac Signs

We know that human sexual behavior has been studied at length. Entire libraries have been written about it, with the aim of helping us understand ourselves and our partners. But is that even possible? It may not be; no matter how smart we are, when it comes to love and sex, there is always an infinite amount to learn. But we have to strive for perfection, and astrology, with its millennia of research, twelve astrological types, and twelve zodiac signs, may hold the key. Below, you will find a brief and accurate description of each zodiac sign's characteristics in love, for both men and women.

Men

ARIES

Aries men are not particularly deep or wise, but they make up for it in sincerity and loyalty. They are active, even aggressive lovers, but a hopeless romantic may be lurking just below the surface. Aries are often monogamous and chivalrous men, for whom there is only one woman (of course, in her absence, they can sleep around with no remorse). If the object of your affection is an Aries, be sure to give him a lot of sex, and remember that for an Aries, when it comes to sex, anything goes. Aries cannot stand women who are negative or disheveled. They need someone energetic, lively, and to feel exciting feelings of romance.

The best partner for an Aries is Cancer, Sagittarius, or Leo. Aquarius can also be a good match, but the relationship will be rather friendly in nature. Partnering with a Scorpio or Taurus will be difficult, but they can be stimulating lovers for an Aries. Virgos are good business contacts, but a poor match as lovers or spouses.

TAURUS

A typical Taurean man is warm, friendly, gentle, and passionate, even if he doesn't always show it. He is utterly captivated by the beauty of the female body, and can find inspiration in any woman. A Taurus has such excess physical and sexual prowess, that to him, sex is a way to relax and calm down. He is the most passionate and emotional lover of the Zodiac, but he expects his partner to take the initiative, and if she doesn't, he will easily find someone else. Taureans rarely divorce, and are true to the end – if not sexually, at least spiritually. They are secretive, keep their cards close, and may have secret lovers. If a Taurus does not feel a deep emotional connection with someone, he won't be shy to ask her friends for their number. He prefers a voluptuous figure over an athletic or skinny woman.

The best partners for a Taurus are Cancer, Virgo, Pisces, or Scorpio. Sagittarius can show a Taurus real delights in both body and spirit, but they are unlikely to make it down the aisle. They can have an interesting relationship with an Aquarius – these signs are very different, but sometimes can spend their lives together. They might initially feel attracted to an Aries, before rejecting her.

GEMINI

The typical Gemini man is easygoing and polite. He is calm, collected, and analytical. For a Gemini, passion is closely linked to intellect, to the point that they will try to find an explanation for their actions before carrying them out. But passion cannot be explained, which scares a Gemini, and they begin jumping from one extreme to the other. This is why you will find more bigamists among Geminis than any other sign of the Zodiac. Sometimes, Gemini men even have two families, or divorce and marry several times throughout the course of their lives. This may be because they simply can't let new and interesting experiences pass them by. A Gemini's wife or lover needs to be smart, quick, and always looking ahead. If she isn't, he will find a new object for his affection.

Aquarians, Libras, and Aries make good partners for a Gemini. A Sagittarius can be fascinating for him, but they will not marry before he reaches middle age, as both partners will be fickle while they are younger. A Gemini and Scorpio are likely to be a difficult match, and the Gemini will try to wriggle out of the Scorpio's tight embrace. A Taurus will be an exciting sex partner, but their partnership won't be for long, and the Taurus is often at fault.

CANCER

Cancers tend to be deep, emotional individuals, who are both sensitive and highly sexual. Their charm is almost mystical, and they know how to use it. Cancers may be the most promiscuous sign of the Zodiac, and open to absolutely anything in bed. Younger Cancers look for women who are more mature, as they are skilled lovers. As they age, they look for someone young enough to be their own daughter, and delight in taking on the role of a teacher. Cancers are devoted to building a family and an inviting home, but once they achieve that goal, they are likely to have a wandering eye. They will not seek moral justification, as they sincerely believe it is simply something everyone does. Their charm works in such a way that women are deeply convinced they are the most important love in a Cancer's life, and that circumstances are the only thing preventing them from being together. Remember that a Cancer man is a master manipulator, and will not be yours unless he is sure you have throngs of admirers. He loves feminine curves, and is turned on by exquisite fragrances. Cancers don't end things with old lovers, and often go back for a visit after a breakup. Another type of Cancer is rarer – a faithful friend, and up for anything in order to provide for his wife and children. He is patriotic and a responsible worker.

Scorpios, Pisces, and other Cancers are a good match. A Taurus can make for a lasting relationship, as both signs place great value on family and are able to get along with one another. A Sagittarius will result in fights and blowouts from the very beginning, followed by conflicts and breakups. The Sagittarius will suffer the most. Marriage to an Aries isn't off the table, but it won't last very long.

LEO

A typical Leo is handsome, proud, and vain, with a need to be the center of attention at all times. They often pretend to be virtuous, until they are able to actually master it. They crave flattery, and prefer women who comply and cater to them. Leos demand unconditional obedience, and constant approval. When a Leo is in love, he is fairly sexual, and capable of being devoted and faithful. Cheap love affairs are not his thing, and Leos are highly aware of how expensive it is to divorce. They make excellent fathers. A Leo's partner needs to look polished and well-dressed, and he will not tolerate either frumpiness or nerds.

Aries, Sagittarius, and Gemini make for good matches. Leos are often very beguiling to Libras; this is the most infamous astrological "master-slave" pairing. Leos are also inexplicably drawn to Pisces – this is the only sign capable of taming them. A Leo and Virgo will face a host of problems sooner or later, and they might be material in nature. The Virgo will attempt to conquer him, and if she does, a breakup is inevitable.

VIRGO

Virgo is a highly intellectual sign, who likes to take a step back and spend his time studying the big picture. But love inherently does not lend itself to analysis, and this can leave Virgos feeling perplexed. While Virgo is taking his time, studying the object of his affection, someone else will swoop in and take her away, leaving him bitterly disappointed. Perhaps for that reason, Virgos tend to marry late, but once they are married, they remain true, and hardly ever initiate divorce. In bed, they are modest and reserved, as they see sex as some sort of quirk of nature, designed solely for procreation. Most Virgos have a gifted sense of taste, hearing, and smell. They cannot tolerate pungent odors and can be squeamish; they believe their partners should always take pains to be very clean. Virgos usually hate over-the-top expressions of love, and are immune to sex as a mean s of control. Many Virgos are stingy and more appropriate as husbands than lovers. Male Virgos tend to be monogamous, though if they are unhappy or disappointed with their partner, they may begin to look for comfort elsewhere and often give in to drunkenness.

Taurus, Capricorn, and Scorpio make the best partners for a Virgo. They may feel inexplicable attraction for Aquarians. They will form friendships with Aries, but rarely will this couple make it down the aisle. With Leos, be careful – this sign is best as a lover, not a spouse.

LIBRA

Libra is a very complex, wishy-washy sign. They are constantly seeking perfection, which often leaves them in discord with the reality around them. Libra men are elegant and refined, and expect no less from their partner. Many Libras treat their partners like a beautiful work of art, and have trouble holding onto the object of their affection. They view love itself as a very abstract concept, and can get tired of the physical aspect of their relationship. They are much more drawn to intrigue and the chase- dreams, candlelit evenings, and other symbols of romance. A high percentage of Libra men are gay, and they view sex with other men as the more elite option. Even when Libras are unhappy in their marriages, they never divorce willingly. Their wives might leave them, however, or they might be taken away by a more decisive partner.

Aquarius and Gemini make the best matches for Libras. Libra can also easily control an independent Sagittarius, and can easily fall under the influence of a powerful and determined Leo, before putting all his strength and effort into breaking free. Relationships with Scorpios are difficult; they may become lovers, but will rarely marry.

SCORPIO

Though it is common to perceive Scorpios as incredibly sexual, they are, in fact, very unassuming, and never brag about their exploits. They will, however, be faithful and devoted to the right woman. The Scorpio man is taciturn, and you can't expect any tender words from him, but he will defend those he loves to the very end. Despite his outward control, Scorpio is very emotional; he needs and craves love, and is willing to fight for it. Scorpios are incredible lovers, and rather than leaving them tired, sex leaves them feeling energized. They are always sexy, even if they aren't particularly handsome. They are unconcerned with the ceremony of wooing you, and more focused on the act of love itself.

Expressive Cancers and gentle, amenable Pisces make the best partners. A Scorpio might also fall under the spell of a Virgo, who is adept at taking the lead. Sparks might fly between two Scorpios, or with a Taurus, who is perfect for a Scorpio in bed. Relationships with Libras, Sagittarians, and Aries are difficult.

SAGITTARIUS

Sagittarian men are lucky, curious, and gregarious. Younger Sagittarians are romantic, passionate, and burning with desire to experience every type of love. Sagittarius is a very idealistic sign, and in that search for perfection, they tend to flit from one partner to another, eventually forgetting what they were even looking for in the first place. A negative Sagittarius might have two or three relationships going on at once, assigning each partner a different day of the week. On the other hand, a positive Sagittarius will channel his powerful sexual energy into creativity, and take his career to new heights. Generally speaking, after multiple relationships and divorces, the Sagittarian man will conclude that his ideal marriage is one where his partner is willing to look the other way.

Aries and Leo make the best matches for a Sagittarius. He might fall under the spell of a Cancer, but would not be happy being married to her. Gemini can be very intriguing, but will only make for a happy marriage after middle age, when both partners are older and wiser. Younger Sagittarians often marry Aquarian women, but things quickly fall apart. Scorpios can make for an interesting relationship, but if the Sagittarius fails to comply, divorce is inevitable.

CAPRICORN

Practical, reserved Capricorn is one of the least sexual signs of the Zodiac. He views sex as an idle way to pass the time, and something he can live without, until he wants to start a family. He tends to marry late, and almost never divorces. Young Capricorns are prone to suppressing their sexual desires, and only discover them later in life, when they have already achieved everything a real man needs – a career and money. We'll be frank – Capricorn is not the best lover, but he can compensate by being caring, attentive, and showering you with valuable gifts. Ever cautious, Capricorn loves to schedule his sexual relationships, and this is something partners will just have to accept. Women should understand that Capricorn needs some help relaxing – perhaps with alcohol. They prefer inconspicuous, unassuming women, and run away from a fashion plate.

The best partners for a Capricorn are Virgo, Taurus, or Scorpio. Cancers might catch his attention, and if they marry, it is likely to be for life. Capricorn is able to easily dominate Pisces, and Pisces-Capricorn is a well-known "slave and master" combination. Relationships with Leos tend to be erratic, and they are unlikely to wed. Aries might make for a cozy family at first, but things will cool off quickly, and often, the marriage only lasts as long as Capricorn is unwilling to make a change in his life.

AQUARIUS

Aquarian men are mercurial, and often come off as peculiar, unusual, or aloof, and detached. Aquarians are turned on by anything novel or strange, and they are constantly looking for new and interesting people. They are stimulated by having a variety of sexual partners, but they consider this to simply be normal life, rather than sexually immoral. Aquarians are unique – they are more abstract than realistic, and can be cold and incomprehensible, even in close relationships. Once an Aquarius gets married, he will try to remain within the realm of decency, but often fails. An Aquarian's partners need uncommon patience, as nothing they do can restrain him. Occasionally, one might encounter another kind of Aquarius – a responsible, hard worker, and exemplary family man.

The best matches for an Aquarius are female fellow Aquarians, Libras, and Sagittarians. When Aquarius seeks out yet another affair, he is not choosy, and will be happy with anyone.

PISCES

Pisces is the most eccentric sign of the Zodiac. This is reflected in his romantic tendencies and sex life. Pisces men become very dependent on those with whom they have a close relationship. Paradoxically, they are simultaneously crafty and childlike when it comes to playing games, and they are easily deceived. As a double bodied sign, Pisces rarely marry just once, as they are very sexual, easily fall in love, and are constantly seeking their ideal. Pisces are very warm people, who love to take care of others and are inclined toward "slave-master" relationships, in which they are the submissive partner. But after catering to so many lovers, Pisces will remain elusive. They are impossible to figure out ahead of time – today, they might be declaring their love for you, but tomorrow, they may disappear – possibly forever! To a Pisces, love is a fantasy, illusion, and dream, and they might spend their whole lives in pursuit of it. Pisces who are unhappy in love are vulnerable to alcoholism or drug addiction.

Cancer and Scorpio make the best partners for a Pisces. He is also easily dominated by Capricorn and Libra, but in turn will conquer even a queen-like Leo. Often, they are fascinated by Geminis – if they marry, it will last a long time, but likely not forever. Relationships with Aries and Sagittarians are erratic, though initially, things can seem almost perfect.

Women

ARIES

Aries women are leaders. They are decisive, bold, and very protective. An Aries can take initiative and is not afraid to make the first move. Her ideal man is strong, and someone she can admire. But remember, at the slightest whiff of weakness, she will knock him off his pedestal. She does not like dull, whiny men, and thinks that there is always a way out of any situation. If she loves someone, she will be faithful. Aries women are too honest to try leading a double life. They are possessive, jealous, and not only will they not forgive those who are unfaithful, their revenge may be brutal; they know no limits. If you can handle an Aries, don't try to put her in a cage; it is best to give her a long leash. Periodically give her some space – then she will seek you out herself. She is sexual, and believe that anything goes in bed.

Her best partners are a Sagittarius or Leo. A Libra can make a good match after middle age, once both partners have grown wiser and settled down a bit. Gemini and Aquarius are only good partners during the initial phase, when everything is still new, but soon enough, they will lose interest in each other. Scorpios are good matches in bed, but only suitable as lovers.

TAURUS

Taurean women possess qualities that men often dream about, but rarely find in the flesh – they are soft, charming, practical, and reliable – they are very caring and will support their partner in every way. A Taurus is highly sexual, affectionate, and can show a man how to take pleasure to new heights. She is also strong and intense. If she is in love, she will be faithful. But when love fades away, she might find someone else on the side, though she will still fight to save her marriage, particularly if her husband earns good money. A Taurus will not tolerate a man who is disheveled or disorganized, and anyone dating her needs to always be on his toes. She will expect gifts, and likes being taken to expensive restaurants, concerts, and other events. If you argue, try to make the first peace offering, because a Taurus finds it very hard to do so – she might withdraw and ruminate for a long time. Never air your dirty laundry; solve all your problems one-on-one.

Scorpio, Virgo, Capricorn, and Cancer make the best matches. A relationship with an Aries or Sagittarius would be difficult. There is little attraction between a Taurus and a Leo, and initially Libras can make for a good partner in bed, but things will quickly cool off and fall apart. A Taurus and Aquarius make an interesting match – despite the difference in signs, their relationships are often lasting, and almost lifelong.

GEMINI

Gemini women are social butterflies, outgoing, and they easily make friends, and then break off the friendship, if people do not hold their interest. A Gemini falls in love hard, is very creative, and often fantasizes about the object of her affection. She is uninterested in sex without any attachment, loves to flirt, and, for the most part, is not particularly affectionate. She dreams of a partner who is her friend, lover, and a romantic, all at once. A Gemini has no use for a man who brings nothing to the table intellectually. That is a tall order, so Geminis often divorce and marry several times. Others simply marry later in life. Once you have begun a life together, do not try to keep her inside – she needs to travel, explore, socialize, attend events and go to the theater. She cannot tolerate possessive men, so avoid giving her the third degree, and remember that despite her flirtatious and social nature, she is, in fact, faithful – as long as you keep her interested and she is in love. Astrologists believe that Geminis do not know what they need until age 29 or 30, so it is best to hold off on marriage until then.

Leo and Libra make the best matches. A relationship with a Cancer is likely, though complex, and depends solely on the Cancer's affection. A Gemini and Sagittarius can have an interesting, dynamic relationship, but these are two restless signs, which might only manage to get together after ages 40-45, once they have had enough thrills out of life and learned to be patient. Relationships with a Capricorn are very difficult, and almost never happen. The honeymoon stage can be wonderful with a Scorpio, but each partner will eventually go their own way, before ending things. A Gemini and Pisces union can also be very interesting – they are drawn to each other, and can have a wonderful relationship, but after a while, the cracks start to show and things will fall apart. An Aquarius is also not a bad match, but they will have little sexual chemistry.

CANCER

Cancers can be divided into two opposing groups. The first includes a sweet and gentle creature who is willing to dedicate her life to her husband and children. She is endlessly devoted to her husband, especially if he makes a decent living and remains faithful. She views all men as potential husbands, which means it is dangerous to strike up a relationship with her if your intentions are not serious; she can be anxious and clingy, sensitive and prone to crying. It is better to break things to her gently, rather than directly spitting out the cold, hard truth. She wants a man who can be a provider, though she often earns well herself. She puts money away for a rainy day, and knows how to be thrifty, for the sake of others around her, rather than only for herself. She is an excellent cook and capable of building an inviting home for her loved ones. She is enthusiastic in bed, a wonderful wife, and a caring mother.

The second type of Cancer is neurotic, and capable of creating a living hell for those around her. She believes that the world is her enemy, and manages to constantly find new intrigue and machinations.

Another Cancer, Virgo, Taurus, Scorpio, and Pisces make the best matches. A Cancer can often fall in love with a Gemini, but eventually, things will grow complicated, as she will be exhausted by a Gemini's constant mood swings and cheating. A Cancer and Sagittarius will initially have passionate sex, but things will quickly cool off. A relationship with a Capricorn is a real possibility, but only later in life, as while they are young, they are likely to fight and argue constantly. Cancer can also have a relationship with an Aries, but this will not be easy.

LEO

Leos are usually beautiful or charming, and outwardly sexual. And yet, appearances can be deceiving – they are not actually that interested in sex. Leo women want to be the center of attention and men running after them boosts their self-esteem, but they are more interested in their career, creating something new, and success than sex. They often have high-powered careers and are proud of their own achievements. Their partners need to be strong; if a Leo feels a man is weak, she can carry him herself for a while- before leaving him. It is difficult for her to find a partner for life, as chivalrous knights are a dying breed, and she is not willing to compromise. If you are interested in a Leo, take the initiative, admire her, and remember that even a queen is still a woman. Timid men or tightwads need not apply. Leos like to help others, but they don't need a walking disaster in their life. If they are married and in love, they are usually faithful, and petty gossip isn't their thing. Leo women make excellent mothers, and are ready to give their lives to their children. Their negative traits include vanity and a willingness to lie, in order to make themselves look better.

Sagittarius, Aries, and Libra make the best matches. Leos can also have an interesting relationship with a Virgo, though both partners will weaken each other. Life with a Taurus will lead to endless arguments – both signs are very stubborn, and unwilling to give in. Leos and Pisces are another difficult pair, as she will have to learn to be submissive if she wants to keep him around. A relationship with a Capricorn will work if there is a common denominator, but they will have little sexual chemistry. Life with a Scorpio will be turbulent to say the least, and they will usually break up later in life.

VIRGO

Virgo women are practical, clever, and often duplicitous. Marrying one isn't for everyone. She is a neat freak to the point of annoying those around her. She is also an excellent cook, and strives to ensure her children receive the very best by teaching them everything, and preparing them for a bright future. She is also thrifty – she won't throw money around, and, in fact, won't even give it to her husband. She has no time for rude, macho strongmen, and is suspicious of spendthrifts. She will not be offended if you take her to a cozy and modest café rather than an elegant restaurant. Virgos are masters of intrigue, and manage to outperform every other sign of the Zodiac in this regard. Virgos love to criticize everyone and everything; to listen to them, the entire world is simply a disaster and wrong, and only she is the exception to this rule. Virgos are not believed to be particularly sexual, but there are different variations when it comes to this. Rarely, one finds an open-minded Virgo willing to try anything, and who does it all on a grand scale – but she is rather the exception to this general rule.

The best matches for a Virgo are Cancer, Taurus, and Capricorn. She also can get along well with a Scorpio, but will find conflict with Sagittarius. A Pisces will strike her interest, but they will rarely make it down the aisle. She is often attracted to an Aquarius, but they would drive each other up the wall were they to actually marry. An Aries forces Virgo to see another side of life, but here, she will have to learn to conform and adapt.

LIBRA

Female Libras tend to be beautiful, glamorous, or very charming. They are practical, tactical, rational, though they are adept at hiding these qualities behind their romantic and elegant appearance. Libras are drawn to marriage, and are good at imagining the kind of partner they need. They seek out strong, well-off men and are often more interested in someone's social status and bank account than feelings. The object of their affection needs to be dashing, and have a good reputation in society. Libras love expensive things, jewelry, and finery. If they are feeling down, a beautiful gift will instantly cheer them up. They will not tolerate scandal or conflict, and will spend all their energy trying to keep the peace, or at least the appearance thereof. They do not like to air their dirty laundry, and will only divorce in extreme circumstances. They are always convinced they are right and react to any objections as though they have been insulted. Most Libras are not particularly sexual, except those with Venus or the Moon in Scorpio.

Leos, Geminis, and Aquarians make good matches. Libra women are highly attracted to Aries men - this is a real case of opposites attract. They can get along with a Sagittarius, though he will find that Libras are too proper and calm. Capricorn, Pisces, and Cancer are all difficult matches. Things will begin tumultuously with a Taurus, before each partner goes his or her own way.

SCORPIO

Scorpio women may appear outwardly restrained, but there is much more bubbling below the surface. They are ambitious with high self-esteem, but often wear a mask of unpretentiousness. They are the true power behind the scenes, the one who holds the family together, but never talk about it. Scorpios are strong-willed, resilient, and natural survivors. Often, Scorpios are brutally honest, and expect the same out of those around them. They do not like having to conform, and attempt to get others to adapt to them, as they honestly believe everyone will be better off that way. They are incredibly intuitive, and not easily deceived. They have an excellent memory, and can quickly figure out which of your buttons to push. They are passionate in bed, and their temperament will not diminish with age. When she is sexually frustrated, a Scorpio will throw all of her energy into her career or her loved ones. She is proud, categorical, and "if you don't do it right, don't do it at all" is her motto. Scorpio cannot be fooled, and she will not forgive any cheating. Will she cheat herself? Yes! But it will not break up her family, and she will attempt to keep it a secret. Scorpios are usually attractive to men, even if they are not particularly beautiful. They keep a low profile, though they always figure out their partner, and give them some invisible sign. There is also another, selfish type of Scorpio, who will use others for as long as they need them, before unceremoniously casting them aside.

Taurus is a good match; they will have excellent sexual chemistry and understand each other. Scorpio and Gemini are drawn to each other, but are unlikely to stay together long enough to actually get married. Cancer can be a good partner as well, but Cancers are possessive, while Scorpios do not like others meddling in their affairs, though they can later resolve their arguments in bed. Scorpio and Leo are often found together, but their relationship can also be very complicated. Leos are animated and chipper, while Scorpios, who are much deeper and more stubborn, see Leos as not particularly serious or reliable. One good example of this is Bill (a Leo) and Hillary (a Scorpio) Clinton. Virgo can also make a good partner, but when Scorpio seemingly lacks emotions, he will look for them elsewhere. Relationships with Lira are strange and very rare. Scorpio sees Libra as too insecure, and Libra does not appreciate Scorpio's rigidity. Two Scorpios together make an excellent marriage! Sagittarius and Scorpio are unlikely to get together, as she will think he is shallow and rude. If they do manage to get married, Scorpio's drive and persistence is the only thing that will make the marriage last. Capricorn is also not a bad match, and while Scorpio finds Aquarius attractive, they will rarely get married, as they are simply speaking different languages! Things are alright with a Pisces, as both signs are emotional, and Pisces can let Scorpio take the lead when necessary.

SAGITTARIUS

Sagittarius women are usually charming, bubbly, energetic, and have the gift of gab. They are kind, sincere, and love people. They are also straightforward, fair, and very ambitious, occasionally to the point of irritating those around them. But telling them something is easier than not telling them, and they often manage to win over their enemies. Sagittarius tends to have excellent intuition, and she loves to both learn and teach others. She is a natural leader, and loves taking charge at work and at home. Many Sagittarian women have itchy feet, and prefer all kinds of travel to sitting at home. They are not particularly good housewives – to be frank, cooking and cleaning is simply not for them. Their loved ones must learn to adapt to them, but Sagittarians themselves hate any pressure. They are not easy for men to handle, as Sagittarians want to be in charge. Sagittarius falls in love easily, is very sexual and temperamental, and may marry multiple times. Despite outward appearances, Sagittarius is a very lonely sign. Even after she is married with children, she may continue living as if she were alone; you might say she marches to the beat of her own drum. Younger

Sagittarians can be reckless, but as they mature, they can be drawn to religion, philosophy, and the occult.

Aries and Leo make the best matches, as Sagittarius is able to bend to Leo's ways, or at least pretend to. Sagittarians often end up with Aquarians, but their marriages do not tend to be for the long haul. They are attracted to Geminis, but are unlikely to marry one until middle age, when both signs have settled down. Sagittarius and Cancer have incredible sexual chemistry, but an actual relationship between them would be tumultuous and difficult. Capricorn can make a good partner- as long as they are able to respect each other's quirks. Sagittarius rarely ends up with a Virgo, and while she may often meet Pisces, things are unlikely to go very far.

CAPRICORN

Capricorn women are conscientious, reliable, organized, and hard-working. Many believe that life means nothing but work, and live accordingly. They are practical, and not particularly drawn to parties or loud groups of people. But if someone useful will be there, they are sure to make an appearance. Capricorn women are stingy, but not as much as their male counterparts. They are critical of others, but think highly of themselves. Generally, they take a difficult path in life, but thanks to their dedication, perseverance, and willingness to push their own limits, they are able to forge their own path, and by 45 or 50, they can provide themselves with anything they could want. Capricorn women have the peculiarity of looking older than their peers when they are young, and younger than everyone else once they have matured. They are not particularly sexual, and tend to be faithful partners. They rarely divorce, and even will fight until the end, even for a failed marriage. Many Capricorns have a pessimistic outlook of life, and have a tendency to be depressed. They are rarely at the center of any social circle, but are excellent organizers. They have a very rigid view of life and love, and are not interested in a fling, as marriage is the end goal. As a wife, Capricorn is simultaneously difficult and reliable. She is difficult because of her strict nature and difficulty adapting. But she will also take on all the household duties, and her husband can relax, knowing his children are in good hands.

Taurus, Pisces, and Scorpio make good matches. Aries is difficult, once things cool off after the initial honeymoon. When a Capricorn meets another Capricorn, they will be each other's first and last love. Sagittarius isn't a bad match, but they don't always pass the test of time. Aquarius and Capricorn are a difficult match, and rarely found together. Things are too dull with a Virgo, and while Leo can be exciting at first, things will fall apart when he begins showing off. Libra and Aquarius are both difficult partners for Capricorn, and she is rarely found with either of them.

AQUARIUS

A female Aquarius is very different from her male counterparts. She is calm and keeps a cool head, but she is also affectionate and open. She values loyalty above all else, and is unlikely to recover from any infidelity, though she will only divorce if this becomes a chronic trend, and she has truly been stabbed in the back. She is not interested in her partner's money, but rather, his professional success. She is unobtrusive and trusting, and will refrain from listening in on her partner's phone conversations or hacking into his email. With rare exceptions, Aquarian women make terrible housewives. But they are excellent partners in life – they are faithful, never boring, and will not reject a man, even in the most difficult circumstances. Most Aquarians are highly intuitive, and can easily tell the truth from a lie. They themselves only lie in extreme situations, which call for a "white lie" in order to avoid hurting someone's feelings.

Aquarius gets along well with Aries, Gemini, and Libra. She can also have a good relationship with a Sagittarius. Taurus often makes a successful match, though they are emotionally very different; the same goes for Virgo. Aquarius and Scorpio, Capricorn, or Cancer is a difficult match. Pisces can make a good partner as well, as both signs complement each other. Any relationship with a Leo will be tumultuous, but lasting, as Leo is selfish, and Aquarius will therefore have to be very forgiving.

PISCES

Pisces women are very adaptable, musically inclined, and erotic. They possess an innate earthly wisdom, and a good business sense. Pisces often reinvent themselves; they can be emotional, soft, and obstinate, as well as sentimental, at times. Their behavioral changes can be explained by frequent ups and downs. Pisces is charming, caring, and her outward malleability is very attractive to men. She is capable of loving selflessly, as long as the man has something to love. Even if he doesn't, she will try and take care of him until the very end. Pisces' greatest fear is poverty. They are intuitive, vulnerable, and always try to avoid conflict. They love to embellish the truth, and sometimes alcohol helps with this. Rarely, one finds extremely unbalanced, neurotic and dishonest Pisces, who are capable of turning their loved ones' lives into a living Hell!

Taurus, Capricorn, Cancer, and Scorpio make the best matches. She will be greatly attracted to a Virgo, but a lasting relationship is only likely if both partners are highly spiritual. Any union with a Libra is likely to be difficult and full of conflict. Pisces finds Gemini attractive, and they may have a very lively relationship – for a while. Occasionally, Pisces ends up with a Sagittarius, but she will have to fade into the background and entirely submit to him. If she ends up with an Aquarius, expect strong emotional outbursts, and a marriage that revolves around the need to raise their children.

Tatiana Borsch